Splatters

Splatters

Diane Torgersen

Published 2020
Copyright © 2020 by Diane Torgersen

ISBN # 9781792355387

Printed in the United States of America
Cover painting "Floating to the Top" by Diane Torgersen

*My great appreciation to The Landfall Writers' Group
who read this manuscript along the way and kindly gave
me their feedback and support.*

*A special thank-you, with doo-dad clusters, to Ed Hearn
and Marie Gillis for volunteering to edit so many pieces.*

*This book is dedicated to my best-friend-forever sister.
Without our hysterical laughs together,
I would not have gotten this far.*

CONTENTS

As splatters of rain
form a whole of water,
so memories form a life.
Bryan Lawrence

INTRODUCTION

These stories are more than a focus on a memoir. They are a collection of personal essays that take the reader on a journey through a writer's thoughts. They cover a multitude of observations spread over many years of watching and listening, from the age of two-and-a half to today. It is hoped that you will find something interesting, familiar or just fun to tug you along through the pages.

A Scrapbook

You only live once.
But if you do it right,
once is enough.
Mae West

ALL OF GAUL

He leaned back in his desk-type chair, after he had asked each student to file past the desk and examine his eyebrow with a magnifying glass. He had circled a single white hair with a pencil and declared that it was a 'feather'. We were to examine this phenomenon and vote with our opinion as to whether this was a feather. Or not.

He was one of the football coaches and was substituting in our chemistry class. Now, I think he either didn't know much about chemistry or was just feeling lazy that day and was more of a mind to entertain or be entertained. Being a single guy, perhaps he had just found a new way to get the girls up close. Really close. He might have become bored, being around the young guys most of the time, and the girls probably smelled better than the locker rooms.

I've thought about that performance many times over the years and still remember puzzling over what he was doing at the time and why, even now. That has brought to mind some of the personalities of other teachers.

I liked my Home Economics instructor. She was deadly serious about what she taught and nurtured us finitely. I remember her saying, after my several attempts to install a zipper according to her standards, "Diane, you have to WANT to put a zipper in before you can do it." I have found over the years that her proclamation fit most situations. Sewing or otherwise. Her personal appearance was important to all of us. She was immaculate with every hair in place. Her make-up was perfect, clothing subdued but well-done. I think her personality was much the same, subdued but caring, kind and watchful. I had just an over-all impression after two years with her, but the best moment that really stands out was the zipper proclamation.

For some reason, I was not a friend of the basketball coach. He also taught physics and economics. I would have liked to have been his friend, but he seemed to take a personal offense at my presence. I didn't play sports, so I didn't have that in common with him and I wasn't in any of his classes. The only time I was in a room with him was when he substituted for another teacher. My best memory of him was when he babysat a class as we took our final chemistry exam. I worked out the problems, answered the questions and was the first to turn in my paper. He took it from me, threw it into the wastebasket and said, "You finished too fast."

I reached into the basket, picked up my exam and left the room. I took the problem to the principal's office. I explained what had happened, and he called the teacher to come in after the exam was over. He asked the coach to grade the paper in front of me. The only corrections he could find were for punctuation and grammar, and he was forced to mark the paper with a 91%. I have no idea why he behaved that way towards me, but in that moment, I found I had an ally and new friend in the principal.

There were two English instructors. One was jolly, friendly, motherly, easily distracted, and we probably were unmerciful to her in our pranks and fun. We knew she loved us, and we got away with everything. In fact, she signed her message in our yearbooks as 'Mom'. Fortunately, she was balanced by the second English teacher who was stern, plodding, on a mission to teach and offered swift retribution for any infractions in her class. We did learn the functioning mechanics of English best from her.

I believe the school's best friend to everyone was the physical education and health instructor. He was approachable to anyone. You knew you could talk to him about anything, and he would be helpful if he could. He had a wicked sense of humor and a knack for encouraging. I had the pleasure of meeting him again at one of our class reunions when he was in his eighties. I told him I was going to do something I had always wanted to do, now being in my fifties. I gave him a hug and a kiss! Even the boys lined up to do the same.

The principal was a fine man, who seemed to look older than he probably was. He was always dressed in a suit, which caused me to wonder, did he take off his jacket when he had to beat someone with the school paddle? Paddling was still done in those days. I don't ever recall anyone saying that he was unfair in his treatment of us, and somehow, he stayed below the radar of serious criticisms. He had a low-wattage sense of humor, but I sensed he was keenly aware of the nonsense of teen behavior and somehow it hit his funny bone in a nice way.

One of my favorites was the Latin teacher. I struggled through two years of her best attempts to make a difference in my understanding of Roman words, because it was my hope to become a doctor. I did manage to pass both years, they were not some of my best grades. I am forever grateful for having taken the classes, now realizing the difference it probably made for my love of words and curiosity in knowing the roots from which they came. Her generosity of personality and awareness of us was genuine. I remember an overall bad day I was having, and I still had to get through her exam. She stopped by my desk in the middle of the test and massaged my shoulders for a moment. I was touched by that gesture and remember it to this day. She said to us many times, "To thine own self be true, and it will follow as night the day, thou canst be false to no man." Her up-right, up-tight, knees-together morality have been memorable to me for many years.

And she told us, "If you remember nothing else from this class, you will always remember, 'All of Gaul is divided into three parts'. In Latin.

Allia Gallia est divesa tres partes. The translation is mine. And so, I did.

Out of Body Beauty

I'd never been there before, but it had been recommended. A pleasant salon where you could have your toes and fingernails repaired and made acceptable for public viewing. The shop keepers were Asian but spoke a lovely accented English.

"Pick a color," I was told. I was then escorted to a chair to have my toes pedicured. The men and women technicians were all friendly, and I had the feeling of being welcomed into their shop circle. Each was smiling and chatting across the room, including me by further smiles and nods, making the experience very family familiar.

The routine was pleasant. Was the water too warm? Do you want the chair adjusted? Some water? A magazine? "No, thank you—I brought a book." There was a little more conversation that was surprisingly interesting and personal, such as the technician was in college, the recent Festival and comments on a magazine that was nearby, until we both drifted into our tasks of reading and pumicing.

It turned out that there might have been an important

alignment of planets there which involved the recorded, piped-in music which was mostly the Carpenters, Streisand, and Beach Boys genre, music of the 50s to 70s. I think the people in the shop had heard the songs so often they were all subconsciously tuned in and involved with it, doing solos and harmonies, softly, together ... alone. Sometimes, one would do a little impromptu dance down the middle of the floor, unconscious of his or her actions. At some points in the renditions, they all joined in together, all over the shop with head or arm or shoulder actions to emphasize the lyrics. Or they just muttered the words that came to the surface as they worked and listened.

I was mesmerized. I felt as if I had walked through The Looking Glass. My imagination began working overtime: What if? Imagine a chorus line of dancers with tuxedo-style costumes: hats, canes, spontaneously dancing together to the words and music down the center of the shop. Then drifting back to their stations of manicures and pedicures, softly singing:

"Imagine you and me ... so happy together.

I can't see me loving nobody but you ... "

Get up and dance for the chorus, back to the customers for the lyrics ...

"And you for me ...

So happy together."

Ending up with ten perfect toes or nails plus a Broadway Revue. Pay the salon. Tip the technician. Drift out the door, back to your life ...

Refreshed.

SPYDER-FIGHTER

At least, that's what I think he should have put on some
vanity license plates, for his big Ram truck. My son has been
a spider-fighter for as long as I can remember. Being a former
Marine, he has gotten very specialized and equipped to do war
with them. You can see his face, demeanor or posture change
when he sees that they have arranged themselves into new col-
onies, or rebuilt webs or found new places to infiltrate. He
comes into the house and announces, "I'm getting The Pig!"
That is a line from the movie "Reds" in which one of the actors
announces his sudden intention to annihilate encroaching
enemies with a special weapon.

It is a dangerous undertaking. He's the only person I know
who has been bitten regularly by the enemy. Not just nips,
either. They can leave gashes that appear to have been chewed.

He sees them in places that I seldom notice, under leaves,
hanging on trees, under the porch ceilings, in the house, dangling from everywhere. Honestly, I'm just as happy not to see

them, or I would be looking for a spider-less, sterile environment in which to move.

But he looks after his Mom and is always willing to do battle around my property. He often looks like one of the Ghostbusters with a white canister and spray nozzle, searching out the fiendish critters. I honesty see spider webs back in place three hours after he has smashed and/or dismantled them. How DO they do that? They seem to be very militant regarding his efforts to eradicate every one of them. He's very thorough about identifying and spraying, but I see the spiders clinging tenaciously to their homes while he squirts and leaves their webs dripping.

He appears to be on the radar of the espionage site of Wolf Spiders. They seem to have identified him as a constant threat and have somehow managed to become larger. Maybe they have little training camps, and special diets to increase their size to appear more threatening. It's working. Honestly, I have seen some that he has chased out that look to be five times bigger. Huge things! And I believe they can jump.

Speaking of jumping bugs, one of my worst nightmares are the big wood roaches that show up in the heat of summer. Those suckers can fly! And they are fond of being in the courtyard where I need to walk my dog. It is a confined space with little room for my screaming, swatting and running. Fortunately, he lays down enough spray that I didn't see a single one last summer. Maybe the word is getting out ... NOW HEAR THIS: Stay away from Bellevue ... lots of our friends and relatives are disappearing ... especially in the courtyard.

I am grateful for his diligence.

The last time he was here, the gardener had just blown away all the leaves and put down fresh pine straw. My son moved a section of it with his foot and hundreds of tiny spiders ran out, just from that spot. They apparently are strengthening their numbers with a bigger crop with which to form an army of retaliation. Or maybe they were in the new pine straw. No matter. They now have new re-enforcements.

I remember a couple of years ago, there were huge spiders living and webbing in one of my Carolina spruces. They seemed to be laying eggs in pods everywhere, on each limb. We finally caught up with a horticulturist who identified the pods as the new seed suppliers for the trees. My son was greatly relieved. It DID look as though the spiders had figured out new armor to use, especially made to protect their unborn.

Back to the huge spiders. They used that tree as their staging ground to intimidate my son and his weaponry. They strung huge, thick webs from the spruce to the neighboring redbuds. As soon as he would knock or tear them down, they were almost immediately replaced. We never saw them at work, but there the repaired webs were, more thickly strung together, more side by side. We both stood and looked at them, hardly believing what the spiders had done. And we never caught them at it. But it didn't matter, he sprayed that tree like there was no tomorrow. At least, for spiders. I never saw another one living there.

Over the years, I think he has found their modular assassin pods with combat training camps and keeps them well sprayed. It's like I have a spider-proof glass dome over my property.

For now, we are just hoping that the spider and flying roach factions don't join forces for Bellevue inter-galactic dominance.

Strangeness and Goodness Nearby

We're all individuals and live among other individuals, each of us having the habits and thoughts that have knit us into the people we have become. It's hard enough to find a mate you are compatible with, let alone buy or rent next to a totally unknown combination of chromosomes, ideologies, and choices with favorite quirks who live next door.

I have lived next door to or near some sweethearts over the years. One comes to mind while in Alaska. We lived next to an Air Force pilot and his wife. That wonderful man used to fill his helmet with fresh tomatoes from nearby fields, when he made trips to the lower forty-eight states and shared them with us. You need to know that totally fresh produce was hard to come by in Alaska. Even in the summer, which had a growing season of about three months, the Anchorage area produced awesomely sized fruits and vegetables that, while pictorially magnificent, tasted bland and diluted. A strawberry could be as big as your fist and carrots as long as your arm and about as thick but still have very little flavor. That is why I remember that sweet soul.

Another was a woman who shared her new baby and her teaching expertise with me, when I was preparing to produce a baby of my own. She invited me to her apartment and gave hands-on tutorials in bathing, dressing and the feeding of small creatures just weeks before my own baby would arrive. What a brave woman she was, because I was totally without skills in that area. She and her husband eventually stationed in Japan, but I was fortunate enough to be her friend again when they later were sent to Alaska. There, she taught me her wonderful and creative baking ideas, her father having been a Norwegian baker. She was a natural-born teacher, and I spent many evenings in her home surrounded by bowls of colored icings and the superb cakes she had made in images of Santa Claus, Easter Bunnies and more.

But the reverse images of those people are the ones that puzzle me.

We lived for a short time next to a house that seemed to thrive on rentals given to the strange and even dangerous. One was a family of five. The wife was a nurse, and the husband was unemployed, possibly deranged or acting out as a public and private abuser. One day, he smeared all her clothes with peanut butter and threw them out the second story window, all while shouting expletives. Their children took kitchen knives outside and I found them chasing my two small boys with them, while shouting what they were going to do to them. That same man attacked my brother and put him in a choke hold, and I, without considering consequences, went after him. Thankfully, someone stopped me. I was eight months pregnant at the time but had forgotten that. Up and down that street was an assortment of abusive situations which included alcoholism, mental health issues and violence, all hidden behind lovely homes and gardens. We put a 'For Sale' sign on our lawn and found a secluded home near a river with mostly friendly people.

Another move was to Texas. My husband was going to a school at the time, and we rented a duplex for the short stay in the town. We had an eighteen-month-old boy and found that our adjoining neighbors had a one-year old girl plus three cats. At the time her husband was in the small base hospital with a bout of hepatitis. The wife seemed eager for a friendship and offered the use of her phone because we didn't have one. I took her up on that one afternoon and knocked on her door to see if it was convenient to make a call. She invited me in, while making chit-chat and preparing her cat's food bowls. Without missing a beat, she put two bowls of cat food on the floor and then set her daughter on the floor. The child crawled over and ate from the bowls, along with the cats.

"That's cat food," I said. "It's ok," she responded, "she likes it."

Her husband was released from the hospital but had to stay home for a while. He made me very uncomfortable in that he would come outside whenever I was out and kept coming closer and closer to where I was. The last time he did it, I was hanging clothes on the outside clotheslines. I turned and walked towards my back door. He began to walk very fast, and I barely got inside the house and latched the door. I shut the main door, telling him that I had work to do. He stood out there, rattling the doorknob, while I hoped it would stay shut.

Scary. Fortunately, he was well enough to return to work soon and my husband finished his classes. We were soon able to leave that location.

Did you ever have your home robbed? It's unsettling, to say the least. I came home from work one day to find my front door standing open. Inside was chaos. My Persian cat was missing, the fridge door standing open, shelves, doors and cabinets were ajar. Clothing was flung from the closets, drawers pulled open, and flowers dumped from their vases onto the floors and furniture. Stolen was the television, a shotgun, small electronics. Other small items were missing and food had been eaten. My cat eventually returned from where she had hidden in the nearby woods.

I called the local police, and they sent people out to investigate and take fingerprints. There had been several robberies in our neighborhood, and they asked to stay in my home the next day because they seemed to think, for some reason, the perpetrators would return. I didn't mind cleaning up the mess of the robbery but cleaning up the graphite from the prints was much harder and very frustrating. The prints were everywhere. Those robbers were eventually identified and caught. One was a young teenager with an even younger friend, both who lived in our small neighborhood.

I went to work the next day and when I told everyone that my home had been robbed, they told me, "You had SAID that you were worried about that happening." As a matter of fact, just the night before, I had gathered all my personal jewelry together and put them into an empty Cool Whip container and set that in the back of the refrigerator. It's the only reason

I have some of those pieces today. Thank goodness, those boys didn't want to top something with Cool Whip.

I have to tell a story about being a neighbor to the British. They were unfailingly kind and uncomplaining. I never heard a cross word with us. But I lived a nervous, how-am-I-doing-with-them kind of life, as their neighbor. Often, we were obliged to have large parties and groups of visiting Americans in our home. I always asked my British neighbors to join us but mostly they graciously declined.

I'm afraid most of the get-togethers were noisy with voices, loud music and perhaps even a lot of the smoke from cigarettes drifted into their homes. Their driveways were often blocked by the big American cars, and there was the noise of our coming and going. I wondered many times what they had thought about the level of the music and loud conversations next door. They seemed to me, to live very quiet lives; I was seldom aware of their being there.

I had a four-year-old and there was a four-year old who lived near us. I have no idea what possessed those boys to do it, but they decided it would be a great idea to hurl stones at my neighbor's brand-new car. Now, the British we knew kept their cars for years and years, nurturing them along into aging car status, due mostly to the cost of replacing them. It became a major statement for my neighbors to have that wonderful new car in their driveway, which was now covered with many stone chips and scratches.

Both of us American families were embarrassed, to say the least, and very upset that it had happened. We assured them that we were going to pay for any repairs or have the car repainted. But no, they repeated over and over that "it was not necessary, and that these things happened." I could see that they were stricken by what had been done to their car. Their property was surrounded by beautiful shrubs and trees that hid the car and yet those two little boys had found it and damaged it. We were never able to convince them to let us repair their car. They were always unfailingly pleasant and cheerful toward us the entire three years we lived next to them. I'm not so sure that if the circumstances were reversed, that we would have behaved as well.

THE LAST OF THE RED-HOT GUNDGE FIGHTERS

I am trying to remember where I was when the story began. It's sort of fuzzy now … probably due to the remnants of cough medications infused with Benadryl. In any case, it was almost six weeks ago. No, wait a minute …… maybe it was five weeks. Let's see, I saw my doctor twice, went to MedAc two times, and that multiplied by 3 and divided by 7 is …… whoops, another cough med malfunction … but I continue.

Long before all that, there was talk on the street of individuals being struck by the sneaky attacks of bronchitis and other flu-like enemies, requiring days of sympathy and various soups brought by loving friends and family members. All from a safe distance, of course. There were days of making phone calls and hearing hoarse, croaky voices on the other end, inquiring who was calling and saying to them, "Would you please call back later, when stricken ones can speak again?"

There seemed to be shaping up a serious frontal attack on our community. Walking our dogs seemed to be a reliable time and source for information gathering. "Did you hear about Jim? He hasn't been out of his house in a week. The neighbors are complaining about the amount and decibel levels of coughing coming from his home." Messages were left on answering machines and phones, asking how afflicted ones were doing while trying to gauge the safety factor in maintaining distances from the house or street. There were quiet underground reports of serious exchanges of medication information being passed around, plus names of reliable humidifier brands and the speed with which Amazon could deliver them to your home.

Some of the first reports seemed to say that most of the afflicted people had some degree of bronchitis, not 'The Flu' which was probably lurking nearby, waiting for its grand entrance. Friends were genuinely agitated now, calling more often to ask "How are you? Have you caught anything yet? Family members doing OK? Do you feel that it is safe to go to the store, movie, and shopping?" Let alone, out to dinner! Anti-bacterial wipes and sprays were disappearing from store shelves at an alarming rate. The restaurants surely noticed a down-turn in business by now. Each evening everyone was in place to listen to the latest local report on television. Was it epidemic yet? Pandemic? All the states were now shaded in the same red, denoting involvement. How about the world? How is 'The World' doing!

One of my neighbors was stricken. We all offered to help by doing her shopping (leaving the packages on the porch, ringing the bell and running), walking the dog (bringing bacterial wipes for leash and hands), after missing her as she was forced to drop out of more and more activities while she struggled back to normal. It was an insidious ailment in that it laid you low, allowed you to feel as if you were recovering then knocked you out of the park again. Hence the array of various types of cough medicines, Mucinex, Benadryl, prescription medications, Tylenol and ibuprofens all lined up on the counters in our homes. You never knew what you were going to be needing next. Are you just getting up and needing to clear everything out of your chest for the day? Do you need to tamp down the amount of coughing and save your body from collapsing into itself? Or are you just hoping to be able to stem the cough and participate in some precious sleep that night? All while sitting propped up on many pillows or sitting in a chair for the duration.

In any case, it is miserable. You miss your life, your friends, and being outdoors while the world isolates itself from you and whatever was causing all this. There is hope. According to the last report, if it is bacterial, antibiotics should have you up and running in a shorter time. If it is viral, you should just pull the foxhole in on top of yourself. It's going to be a long wait.

The Mole and I

Years ago, I was given a remedy by a friend for getting rid of moles. Each time I have used it, it has worked. The idea was to bury an empty glass soda or beer bottle halfway down in the dirt of a mole trail. My friend told me it was the sound of wind blowing across the bottle's opening that made the moles leave.

As I said, each time that I used it, it did what it was supposed to do, whether the moles lived in Maryland, Delaware, Florida or North Carolina. I asked many people over the years why they thought it was successful. No one knew, but they were only happy that it was a solution to the invading, multiplying, destructive and determined moles who were probably only trying to live in peace in their mole trails with their mole families.

I did have a conversation once with a builder about that remedy and he said he had noticed over the years that when he would have land cleared, people in surrounding lots would complain that their yards were suddenly full of traveling moles. He surmised the moles did not like either the noise or the rumbling vibrations of the machinery, let alone having their homes dug up and moved around.

I met my match recently.

I had noticed there was a mole trail across my back court-yard, just inside the garden gate. The gate didn't hit the tunneled-up dirt when I opened and closed it, so it wasn't causing any trouble, but just for the heck of it, I stomped the trail down.

I think that made him cranky.

The next day, the trail was back in place, only it was higher and wider. I flattened the dirt down again and checked the next morning to see if any progress had been made by either of us. There it was, defiantly piled up again. Time for the BOTTLE, I decided. Unfortunately, the only one I could find was a plastic Coke bottle. What the heck, I thought, I'll see if plastic works as well.

The next morning, I could see the mole had pushed the bottle out of the trail. I pushed it down more firmly. In a few hours, it was standing at a rakish angle with dirt piled around it. I pulled the bottle out and planted it at another spot in the trail. The area we were fighting over was only about twenty-eight inches long. The next time he created two (count 'em!), two y-shaped dividing trails away from the bottle. Kind of reminds me of when the posse was chasing Butch Cassidy and the Sundance Kid, and the posse divided into two lines during the night. HOW did the mole do that? Without disturbing the bottle?

I should have looked for a glass bottle to replace the plastic one and continue the argument, but as a parting blow, the mole ate the roots of a newly planted fatsia shrub that was about twelve inches from the end of his work, killing half of it. Probably a warning shot if I wanted to keep the other half. I had to admire his tenacity and resourcefulness in maintaining his territory and making underground statements about his dirt rights and mine.

I now look at the disputed garden area with admiration and a new respect for my tiny foe. 'You win. May the force be with you.'

Transformations
in the '50s

This is a strange time of life, our youth, in which one is trying to struggle across the abyss of two lives. Your body has become an outlaw, sneaking up on you and doing strange things and beginning to behave and look differently to what we were used to. Your usually pleasant emotions and behavior now have two minds. One is still happy sitting at the table eating your Cheerios for breakfast, and the other is suddenly angry at everything and is developing a new language to show the frustration of an encroaching, maybe exciting, New World.

It is a serious time of life. You feel that you are fighting for the past couple of years for a survival you have only noticed and watched from the distance of childhood. You have watched others change before your eyes and now you are searching to find ways to be accepted and acceptable in those groups. You are probably feeling ill-informed and ill-equipped to manage the needs and ideas that are now raging through your quickly changing body and mind.

Think about it, all of a sudden, your clothes no longer fit. Maybe you grew six inches taller in two months, or areas of your body are different. So many changes to get used to! And even the words that we used to use are no longer useful. We need stronger nouns and verbs, and sullen looks to strengthen our positions. Our parents are whispering when we enter a room or slamming down punishments when we overstep the usual boundaries of behavior or language.

You need a friend.

So, you find others that are entering this alien world and compare notes. Magazines and movies have useful information. Studying the older teens, when they will allow you into their air space, is helpful, but then you have even more questions and new areas that you want to be a part of, but those areas now have barriers of dress, language or attitude. This requires research, including studying this new language, clothing, posture and even identifying reactions to what is quickly confronting everyone your age. It all takes time—too long, really, when everything is moving past you at warp-speed and you are shedding your skin of childhood.

Boys have an easier time of it. They seem to just need a pair of cuffed jeans, a white T-shirt, a sullen attitude and a pack of cigarettes rolled up in the sleeve, as signs of their new independence. And one of the new duck-tailed haircuts.

Girls need more experimenting and conversations about everything. Pierced ears are a new and racy idea. Short hair cuts or ponytails are endlessly discussed. The now childish full skirts with flouncy crinolines and sweaters with false collars give way to tight, straight skirts and tighter sweaters to enhance their changing figures, with a statement scarf knotted around the neck. And of course, everyone, including boys, is wearing penny loafers and white crew socks. The uniform has been identified, cataloged and acknowledged. There is safety in uniformity. In the '50s, even sleeveless clothing was considered a little adventurous and frowned upon by some adults. There is also the issue of make-up, the hallmark of stepping into another galaxy. That clearly moved us towards the identity of high school proprieties and away from the stigma of eighth graders. There was much practicing of how to apply it, where to put it, which colors, endless sharing of brands, and carefully hiding our supplies from parents.

It wasn't easy breaking through our chrysalis of childhood into the glittering adult world of teens. But one day we seem to have gotten it right and made the transfer from children to a group of people who all dressed the same, who spoke the same language and were accepted by each other.

I wonder how it works now, when young people are often as strangely different as possible from each other, in appearance and dress, (in comparison to our '50s conformity) with both boys and girls now shaving the sides of their heads, and the abundance of tattoos and pierced bodies. There are also the riots of colors and patterns worn together, often torn into shreds and tatters, not to even mention the influence of drugs and gangs, and the different ways and opinions of considering the idea of morals.

Something nostalgic in me hopes that the transformations are still the same and that now they're just wearing different clothes.

UNCLE

The veranda was shaded by waving palms in the middle of the day. It was so dark that one could barely see the doors and windows of the house and the chairs sitting around in mis-matched places. There was a presence of a wind blowing, but mildly so. It was just enough to stir the heat around and make one aware that even the sand would be uncomfortable for walking. The mild rubbing and dry slashing sounds of the palm fronds moving against each other added to the sense of a slow, sluggish day.

She was looking for her aunt but was cautious about disturbing her uncle who was a known irritant to anyone who came unbidden into his area. She walked slowly but wanted to move faster because the heat of the sand was burning through her sandals.

Where is he? she thought, wanting to mark her uncle's location before walking on. He usually liked to sit outside on the veranda in just his shorts, avoiding the still heat in the open house. She narrowed her eyes against the dark strain of separating shapes in front of her.

In one area she saw something small move. A cat. "Now what is a cat doing here?" she mused out loud. Everyone knew of her uncle's special hatred of all cats. It sat quietly against the wall, under a window and seemed to wait for her to move that way. As she moved closer, the cat came slowly and quietly toward her. She was able to bend down and pick it up. She held it close and felt its small body adjust to her arms and hands. The two just stood there, acknowledging the adjustments they both were making, and the acceptance of each other's decisions at the moment.

What they hadn't noticed was the uncle watching them through one of the windows. His natural coloring helped his image blend into the surrounding darkness of the house and veranda, making him impossible to be seen from their position. He gave them enough time to walk up the steps to the veranda when he pushed the screen door open with a loud bang and a shout, "What in the hell are you doing, bringing that cat into my house!" He banged the door against the house more times and stamped his feet, to make as much noise as possible and growled in her direction.

She felt the cat tighten toward her and felt her own body do the same as she turned toward her menacing uncle. She had seen him in his ugly moods before and had decided that she would never let him scare her again. He was just a mean person. "I'm looking for Aunt Marcy," she said.

"And what are you doing with that damned cat on my property?! You give it to me! Now! I'm going to wring its neck and get rid of it!" he shouted.

"No," she said. "The cat is mine." She stood defiantly before him, and he stared hard at them and seemed to swell to an even larger size.

Just then Aunt Marcy opened the screen door and said, "Leave them alone, Roy, she's just carrying the cat. It isn't in the house and she's going to take it home with her." He stomped his feet again before turning around glaring at her and the cat one more time, muttering under his breath about his hatred of cats. He banged the door again as he entered the house.

It was again quiet in the yard. Aunt Marcy looked at Dena, asking what she was visiting for, and reminded her that Uncle Roy didn't like to be awaken from his naps in the afternoon.

"My birthday is soon," she said. "I'm going to be nine, and I wanted to ask you to make a new dress for me to wear to my party."

For her mental and physical safety, Dena was staying with her grandmother during a time of turbulence in her own family. Marcy was unhappy that Dena had been confronted by her moody and unpredictable husband but didn't want to keep making apologies. "Leave the cat here and come inside so we can talk about what kind of dress you would like. You can take the cat home with you."

Later, when she was ready to leave, they looked for the small cat. They found its little body, lying twisted in the sand by the side of the house. The uncle had made good his promise.

EXPECTATIONS

We had talked about and planned for her trip to North Carolina for months. I had offered her a round-trip plane ticket and asked if she would like to stay a few weeks. My friend and I had not spent more than a few days with each other since leaving school. And ... I wanted to check out our attitudes and temperatures regarding our current ages.

The differences began with her desire to bring a twenty-eight pound terrier mix who was one and a half years old. I encouraged her to consider leaving him with her daughter, a friend or her ex-husband. I offered to pay for a kennel-spa for him there in New Mexico. That would give us more freedom for small trips or perhaps some classes we could take together. I had an eight-year-old Shih Tzu which I comfortably leave at a kennel for short times. She absolutely drew the line with putting her dog on a plane, having heard many horror stories about dogs dying in the plane's hold during the summer. I had to agree, I probably would not be comfortable with that either. So, we decided to abandon the get-together.

But then she decided to drive across country with her dog. Each time I talked to her, the trip had become longer and more circuitous while she added more and more stops. She traveled across New Mexico, Texas, Louisiana, Alabama, Mississippi and into Florida to visit with various cousins, friends, brother, grand-children, great-grandchildren and then on to North Carolina. It took almost two weeks for her to arrive from New Mexico but arrive she did.

I need to say that she is blessed, or cursed, with endless energy. It is impossible for her to be still. If she has to be still, then she begins what I've always called 'clucking and humming'—a singy, talky way of entertaining herself with inflections of up and down sounds that I have noticed hens making while scratching around outside. I have often, over the years, offered her a sizable amount of money to not drink coffee in the mornings. The caffeine-high is incredible along with her natural, built-in caffeine, but she insists she likes this two or three hour-rush, so we just have to wait for her to come down from the chandeliers.

Her dog has the same problem of high energy and constant motion and is an immediate problem. He charges towards my ten-pound Shih Tzu, who has never been terrorized in her life, and he begins shoving his nose under her little body, lifting her off the floor and pushing her along like a snowplow. I pick her up and he lunges for me, almost knocking us over. She is calling his name and yanking on his leash, trying to get him down, until she gets him tethered to a piece of furniture, and that's the way it is.

"They will just have to get used to each other," she pronounces. And I say, "My dog is not going through that again."

Welcome to the first five minutes of being in North Carolina together.

She has had the dog, a pound rescue, for eleven months and hasn't had time to teach him how to obey. No sit, stay, or come. No "don't kill our friend's dog," "don't chew on everything that you can get in your mouth" and "don't include the tops of tables in your racing around the house." She HAS allowed him to develop some of his own fun ideas such as, she allows him to sit behind her in the chair while she sits at a table to eat. THAT was the first of my own proclamations, "there will be no sitting of dogs in chairs at the table while we have meals." He had become skilled at racing around the house at 4:00 P.M. after he gets a protein rush from his evening meal, rattling the dishes in the cabinets, sideswiping whatever is in his path, which she has allowed him to do at home. "He gets so little exercise, otherwise", she explained.

I am still finding pieces of items that he chewed and destroyed, as they began wafting out from under my furniture when the air conditioning came on after they left. My dog no longer has a collection of toys. No matter … she wasn't playing with most of them, anyhow. I did manage to save her favorite 'first toy', her squirrel. I think it was when I was standing in my laundry room, and he was waiting about fifteen feet away in the garage when I saw an apparition of things to come. I called, "Come Jojo." Then I truly realized what kind of trouble I was in. I saw him leap from a standing start, straight into the laundry room, by-passing two steps, and landing three feet inside the room, knocking me into the dryer on his way into the house. That was a force to be reckoned with.

After much trial and error, and after my friend would not agree to a kennel, we decided we would just have to keep the dogs separated. Fortunately, I had a sturdy wire folding fence in the garage and put it up. The dogs took turns being behind it, mostly so my dog could eat and rest in safety. The wolf/terrier patrolled the fence constantly, looking for a way in … or out. I am so thankful he never realized that he probably could have sailed over the fence, after seeing him leap from the garage. Whenever we left the house, we had to lock them both into separate rooms and pray he couldn't get out because I was pretty sure he could batter down my dog's door. I vacillated over taking my own dog to a sitter, but now I was so cross I was determined that he would be the one to leave.

We really couldn't do much because of him. She went walking with him for three hours in the mornings, trying to siphon off some of the energy and aggression and walked him other times during the day. She insisted that the dog's behavior was due to the 'stress' in my home.

Her dog needed some booster shots, so I took them to my vet. She began to tell the vet some of what was going on, asking for advice, and I mentioned that the dog had bitten my son, threatened me and my dog constantly, and frankly, also my friend. The vet simply said he could provide some tranquilizers, and she should probably get a basket muzzle to have ready for the rest of her trip. None of which she thought she would do. The little guy should "run free". She was already tethering him to furniture, or to herself, or locking him in a room. She thought that was sufficient.

She seemed to talk to him constantly, I'm sure to try to

keep him distracted or calm, which did not work. Her voice would go so high that I tracked it on my piano. "Do you know that you talk to him in the key of high-C sharp?" I told her.

Some dog adoptions are good matches, and some are not. He really hadn't been socialized because she lives off the grid in upper New Mexico. There are no other dogs nearby, but lots of coyotes and wolves, so he cannot be left outside. He is either on a leash or inside a building. And since she works, he is left alone much of the time. I do feel sorry for both of them. She has bonded with him and is loath to let him go. I feel that he is dangerous, even to her. When he doesn't get his way, he puts his teeth on you, or lunges at you with a quarterback's-shoulder-into-the-body technique. We finally had to cut our time together short and agree to catch up some other day.

I had added a pint of whiskey to my iced tea, a few tablespoons at a time, over the few days we were together. My son noticed that the bottle was almost empty and raised his eyebrows at me. I just shrugged. That kinda said it all.

Expectations hopefully continue.

RUN! HIDE! BUY SPAM!

Those words written by one of my favorite cartoonists, Jake Vest, could relate to the current pandemic, although it applies to an approaching hurricane being reported on television: Meteorologist Barry Ometer here. I think this is going to be real bad! Run! Hide! Pray! Buy Spam! Nail plywood up at random! Oh, the humanity! (How's my hair?)

I think that seems to fit well with the current panic, indecision, and 'Oh No!' that most are experiencing right now. Leave the gun? Take the cannoli-kind-of-thing. One can only listen to so much of the news until they have to escape over the hill to find other conversations. But alas, it's outside, too. Neighbors trying to define and enact social distancing while bobbing in and out of the restricted zones as they are trying to judge distances between themselves and others, some with masks and some without masks. Like kindergarteners learning new social skills. What's not to understand? Six feet apart, mask on. But we are so used to our habits that it takes a few moments to realize that we have slid way back into the past and are two feet from someone, and they do not have a mask on! Or I don't. Odd that we can't visually recognize it right away.

In the beginning, friends and neighbors were leaving cookies and other good things on each other's porches. What a dilemma that created. How does one quarantine cookies? And the bag or box that they arrived in? And what about the Amazon boxes and plastic grocery bags, let alone the items in them. We finally resorted to putting the frozen things in the freezer, milk, etc. in the fridge and left the bags with usables inside, lined up and down the hall, in quarantine to wait their turn to be unpacked ... in two or three days. I think I ate one of the cookies ahead of time, and then waited to see if I was going to die. It's hard to resist a home-made chocolate chip cookie.

Ok, let's get serious. We have a pandemic going on. We have curfews and the breaking of store windows happening. There is some looting, although that doesn't seem to be a problem locally. We seem to have subliminal instructions to line up in front of our televisions at night to watch the latest window smashage, lootings and increasing crowds. Also, the smacking down of elderly people onto the sidewalks who lie there with their ears bleeding, while the smackee walks away, having already lost interest in their latest protest activity. No one taps them on the shoulder to say, "Hey, you deliberately just knocked someone down. Aren't you even going to look back at him?" as the white-haired fellow just lies there, quietly, on his back. I'm still wondering if he was okay.

I grew up in a generation in which my father called any elderly gentleman "Dad," if he didn't know his name. He was always gentle and careful to determine what their needs were, if any. The action of someone summarily just reaching out of a crowd and knocking an innocent person down would have brought swift retribution from others standing nearby. They probably would have been beaten 'a little' and then taken to the nearest police station where someone knew what to do with them.

What have we become? What has changed in just a generation and in such a short time? There are many seeds that could be named as possibilities. What are your 'seeds'? What is growing around you?

Sharing the World

How did it get
so late so soon?
Dr. Seuss

Enlarging Boundaries

It's a new experience, sitting for fifteen hours, and feeling your plane constantly shake in a shimmy the entire time. Having someone bring you ice cream bars, meals, drinks and having a wall-sized map in front of you with a tiny object moving across an ocean does not make the time pass faster. Nor does it keep you from wondering that if we went down here, how deep IS the water ... not that it would matter.

But the experience and excuse to go to Australia were worth any anxiety over the details of getting there. My husband and I planned months for the adventure. My son was marrying the girl of his dreams in Adelaide, Australia. It was spring in Florida but would be autumn in Adelaide. That caused an odd feeling of having to 'think backwards' ... or forwards. Confusing. I finally found what I thought would be an appropriate outfit to wear as the mother-of-the-groom, which also meant 'will not wrinkle' in a suitcase for a twenty-nine-hour trip.

We arrived in Sydney in time to catch the next flight to Adelaide. I wish I had not been so sleep-deprived. There surely were interesting things going on around me that I was neglecting to notice. Flying over the ocean at night did not encourage me to spend the time sleeping, because I felt I had to watch that little plane on the screen. Nor did the next flight, so I arrived feeling out of touch with the planet and in another reality. Being met at the hotel by a nervous bride-to-be, our son and her three teenage children is still a blur. I had been awake for 36 hours and had spent days and hours beforehand preparing to leave. I think the meeting went well ... the charming Aussie accents did much to delight and the young teens were quickly moving into my heart. The bride and I were obviously curious about each other, stealing quick looks and trying to find mutual areas of conversation. We agreed that we would see each other at dinner that evening.

An older son and his wife who had arrived earlier were already riding around in a jeep in the Outback, with the Best Man and an Aussie relative, to keep them from getting lost.

My overall impression of Adelaide was of being sent in a time machine back to the '50s. That included the appearance of stately buildings, homes, and manner of dressing (my husband and I were receiving quick but polite glances, from the townspeople). We were dressed in jeans, khakis, shirts and jackets with what Australians would call 'trainers' - what now felt to be enormous Mickey Mouse-sized white Nike walking shoes to us. The townspeople were dressed as if they were going to church, and everyone wore leather shoes. That reminded me very much of having lived in England, but Aussies did not like to be called "English." Their good manners reminded me of how people 'used to be' in the '50s. It felt familiar, kinder, and slower than where I had come from.

My son worked for a Japanese company that shipped metro train shells to the United States and outfitted them in Wisconsin. The president of the company and his wife flew from Japan to stay only the day of the wedding. What an honor that was for my son. His wife did not speak English, but she had the bearing of a beautiful Kabuki dancer, and we women tried very hard to find a way to communicate. She was equally curious about us. She looked to be about thirty, but we determined she had six children and was fifty. Most amazing ... and exquisite.

The day of the wedding was properly cold, for it was their 'November' but our 'May' in Florida. The service was much too fast and over much too soon. It was typically lovely, and my son was handsome as was his bride beautiful. We were so busy filming and taking pictures that I'm sure we missed a few things. One of the most memorable moments to me was when we all were standing outside while waiting for the photographer to make the interior shots. I began a conversation with a woman and her husband and on the 'other side of the world' and I found a comrade in study. We both were taking the very same Bible study class—the International Bible Study Fellowship and were on the same page in our classes. We waited for a long time outside where it was so cold, until they offered to take us into their home, which was nearby. As I walked away with them, my husband called me back and reminded me that I had to have pictures taken also. I am still amazed at the continuity, closeness and moments I had with them, on the other side of the world. I felt I had known them forever, and it made sense for me to go with them. We kept up with each other for years through the Internet, but I finally lost track of them when they became missionaries to Africa.

The wedding was sweet and charming. The reception was memorable because it was held in a favorite pub. At some point, I stood and spoke to my son and his bride regarding hardships in life but advised them to remember this remarkable day when those hard days came along. When I sat down, I saw that several people around me were quietly crying and wiping their eyes. "What did I say?" I asked. "I'm not sure ...... but it was beautiful", someone near me said. Oh dear ... next time I will make notes. I do remember that I had the Twenty-third Psalm in my mind while I was talking to them, which does have the line, "Yea, though I walk through the valley of the shadow of death ......" in it. Whoops?

We had made arrangements to stay a few days in Sydney before returning to the States. I had booked us into a hotel downtown, but my husband, new to the Internet, chose to flex his computer muscles by practicing on changing our accommodations to another area. I did not have time to check it closely or argue with what he had done.

We picked up a taxi at the Sydney airport to take us to our new temporary residence and begin to realize that it was taking a long time to reach it. A VERY long time. When we finally arrived in front of it, we realized that we were in a very different kind of area. I think it used to be called a "red light district" in old gangster movies and books. There was a low wall in front of the small apartment building in which we would be staying. Sitting on that wall was a short line of men, some of whom were being affectionate with each other in a manner that we were not used to seeing. It became obvious we must have led a very sheltered life.

We gathered our luggage and trooped up the stairs to check

out our living area, which was not that bad. It was a little down at the heels, but clean. We decided to unpack later and headed out to do some exploring and to look for somewhere to have lunch.

That's when the reality of where we were staying really began to be more apparent. Many of the young men who were walking around had the butt-cheeks of their Levi's cut out, in oval circles, showing lots of bare skin. Some bare bottoms were tattooed. The store fronts were 'very out-spoken' in offering their wares which needed a fair amount of studying to try to determine exactly what they were. It didn't take us long to stop 'studying' them. Most were paintings featured that had various styles of nudity. The men along the street were giving my husband a lot of smiles and winks.

Not feeling extremely safe in the area, we hurried along until we found a taxi to take us into the city proper. We had booked into the apartment for two nights and decided that since the next day was taken up with a long trip into the Outback, we would stay. We did happen to walk by my previous choice of a hotel and found that it would have been perfect. It was in the middle of downtown and close to everything that we would have like to have done. But it wouldn't have been nearly as interesting.

We noticed there was a buffet-type diner diagonal to our apartment, so we decided to have an early breakfast there the next morning. One comforting realization was that the local police department was on the other corner because we did hear what might have been gunshots during the night and some distant yelling.

The expedition to the Outback was spectacular. We were

in a small van with about six other adventurers, and we were looking forward to a ride of a lifetime. There was almost too much to remember clearly. The most memorable was a ride down a very steep mountainside in tiny cars, on a very small track enclosed almost entirely by huge trees on either side. One brave soul tried the cable car slung between two mountain tops. She did not look at all well when she returned. She was still talking and moving around, but very pale and shaky.

One stop was at a zoo with typical Aussie creatures in it. I mostly remember the kangaroos that were all lying around on the sandy ground as if they were ill. It was disturbing to see them. I found someone to ask what was wrong with them, and he said, "Nothing is wrong with 'em. They're just like people. Give 'em enough free food to eat, mate, and they will just lie about, waitin' for the next meal."

The colors and hugeness of just the small area we visited, I will remember forever. It was massive in an enormously quiet way, with not much traffic and not many people around. We stopped for tail-gate lunches near trees that were filled with hundreds of cockatoos. Most of them that I had seen before had been in a cage in someone's home and were very expensive.

An occasional kangaroo hopped through the scenery. A fitting end to our Australian adventure.

MILE MARKER 462

It was 1962. We were making a military move from San Antonio, Texas to Anchorage, Alaska with our eighteen-month-old son and had decided to drive the Alaskan Highway (the ALCAN) for the scenic experience. We made one stop in Wyoming to visit with my parents and then entered Canada to make our way to Mile Marker #1 to begin our journey through the wilderness.

In that year, the road was gravel, filled with big chunks of rocks. There were huge road graders working all the time to keep it evenly spread. The views were magnificent around every bend in the road including mountains, tall pines, northern trees, and gracious panoramas off in the distance around huge boulders and rocks. From our can we could see rivers, streams, deer and bears. Not too many people were traveling then, so it was exciting to pass someone going south. The time of year was May, and the weather was beautiful and getting colder.

I can't tell you how long it would have taken us to drive the entire highway to Anchorage because I was traveling in the 400 series of Mile Markers and hit a rock in the road. At the time, I was driving on the left side of the road because a grader was working on the right. A car was coming towards us, so I crossed over a heap of gravel down the middle of the road to get back into my lane. There just happened to be a huge boulder right there under the gravel that the car tried to climb. The car quickly stopped, hung up on the pile of gravel. The worker on the grader came to try to help us, but nothing seemed to work. We flagged down someone going north to ask that they alert an inn up ahead about five miles that we needed assistance.

After a short time, someone did come. This type of thing apparently happened a lot. They arranged for our car to be towed to Lake Muncho Lodge at mile marker 462 for evaluation. Once there, a mechanic eventually came from one of the far-spaced gas stations along the highway to see if he could help. The diagnosis was that all motor mounts were broken, and the driveshaft was history. It could have been worse. We were in the middle of a proverbial 'no-where' with very few car parts stores. One of the workers at the lodge even asked that the mechanic take the driveshaft off his own car to see if it would fit ours. A gracious gesture, but it didn't work. The motor mounts didn't seem to be the biggest issue. There was nothing to do but contact Detroit and order another driveshaft. We were told it would arrive by bus. That bus only came by once a day.

My husband notified Elmendorf Air Force Base of our predicament and we stayed to wait for the bus each day. We waited anxiously each day to see if our driveshaft had arrived.

Despite our worry about repairing the car, it was a beautiful area for this to have happened. Muncho Lake was across the road with mountains and trees all around although we were warned about bears and other dangerous creatures just out back. The lodge had a bar and restaurant, rustic rooms and surprisingly a very loyal clientele of daily visitors who lived back in the woods and came out for nourishment and drinks with friends. Some of them soon adopted us and took us to the few entertainment spots in the area. One was a hot springs pool of water hidden "way back in the hills."

One afternoon we missed our eighteen-month-old son. We looked in the usual places because he had made himself at home in the lodge and everyone knew him. After a very short time of looking unsuccessfully, we all began to panic. The back door of the kitchen had been left standing open, and we realized that he could have wandered out. A bear had been spotted in the area the night before, and then there was the lake across the street. People began running in all directions trying to find him. We called and called. I was standing in the kitchen trying to catch my breath and think what to do next when I heard a delicate little 'clink'. My son was sitting on the floor behind a big door. There was a crate of empty beer bottles back there, and he was systematically drinking the leftovers and gently putting the bottles back. He took a good nap that day.

After waiting and meeting the daily bus for a week, we ultimately had to finish our trip to Anchorage on the bus. What an experience that was. The driver was part tour guide and would often stop by the road. We could see or watch something going on, such watch as a herd of elk eating in a field, bears ambling along the road or just observe a special, beautiful scene before us. Once he stopped abeam of the Dahl Mountains to see if we could catch a glimpse of the elusive Dahl sheep, which we did. How nice to have someone else doing the driving.

My husband returned about a week later after the car part had arrived, to drive our car on to Anchorage where, for a 1955 Pontiac sedan, it performed in an excellent manner through the 3 years of brutal winters and then we drove it across Canada and back to San Antonio, Texas by way of Tennessee when we changed bases again.

STAY ON THE SHIP

Advertisements of Caribbean cruises can be mesmerizing, especially in the colder months. What's not to like—palm trees, incredible blue-green water, and the colorful houses. The ships offer such a variety of entertainment, dining venues, and opportunities to be experienced. There are the Broadway-worthy performances, exotic lounges, and bistros right along the avenue of the ship's indoor shopping mall. There are swimming areas and work-out rooms, as well as lectures and classes. The staterooms were spacious and quiet with everything done for you, including the nightly towel creations of animals, made by the service personnel. Each day is an extravaganza of choices, starting with a morning sunbath with Calypso music alongside a beautiful pool area, or a quick stroll around the ship's decks, or a massage after a trip to a steam room. Then, there is the eternal buffet on the fantail for 24-hour snacking and the scheduled gourmet meals in themed dining-rooms.

There are seducing onshore excursions available while the ship is in port. We were stopped at a port that offered a bus trip to Panama and a drive alongside the Panama Canal. My husband and I thought that one would be interesting and signed up to leave the next morning, along with about twenty-five other passengers.

While driving beside the Canal, the driver explained parts of it to us. We stopped along the way to see one of the locks up close and watch a ship move through it. Our next stop was to be one of the South American churches. Along the road to visit that one, we could look down from the bus, into the small, almost empty one-room homes alongside the road and see possibly two pieces of furniture, a television and a single electric line, strung through the air, into what looked to be a home with a dirt floor. We passed three story buildings with people standing on balconies. These buildings seemed so old and ancient that they looked as though they might crumble into dust at any moment. It was a very poor and needy country.

We finally arrived at the church and were escorted into it, while someone began telling us about its history. At one point, I whispered to my retired, military husband, "There are men standing around us with rifles." He slowly looked around us but didn't say anything. They were just quietly there. I really wondered if we were going to be kidnapped. There had been reports of that happening recently to Americans. We finally returned to the bus and didn't see the gunmen, but after we arrived in Panama City, there they were again standing around us as we walked through the city with a guide. We were hurried back onto the bus and taken for a lunch to a small restaurant, which I noticed had only one main entrance. The gunmen stood outside the restaurant with their rifles at the ready, while we ate a very mediocre lunch, very quickly, because there seemed to be an unsaid notion to hurry.

When we returned outside to get on our bus, I saw there was now a second bus behind ours. Someone said, "This is a spare, in case you need one." Not a good feeling. It was beginning to look very much like an international incident being avoided. Both buses drove straight through the town. There were military people at each intersection to stop all traffic as we drove through each one, without stopping. Someone wanted us out of town in a hurry. As we got further from the town, the military escort dropped away.

We were a group of very angry Americans when we returned to the ship and headed for the administration office, which had allowed the trip to be planned and demanded to tell the captain what had happened and ask why it had not been deleted. He did come out to meet with us, but nothing was offered other than an apology. It wasn't a good thought to think that we might have been attacked or even held for ransom for a time.

Another reminder that off-ship entertainment is not always a good idea happened when we stopped at a Jamaican port on another cruise. We had been told that we would only be in port a short time, but there was a small shopping area up the road. We were carefully told to only use local taxis that had a certain insignia on the front of their cars. As we walked off the ship, we noticed that there were not many people leaving. We should have paid attention to that fact. We met one couple we knew who were returning from a walk on land while docked and they asked us if we intended to go into the small town.

They advised us to reconsider, saying they had done it one time and it had been a bad idea, but my husband still wanted to make the excursion. He hated to back down after a decision had been made.

We rode about ten minutes into the 'town' which turned out to be just a little strip of shops along the road. Our driver was anxious and said that he would wait for us.

As we walked towards the shops, we could see we were the only visitors there. The people began to slowly crowd around us, pointing to the different shops and encouraging us to 'go over there.' They began a gently nudging and pushing. I was definitely getting nervous and told my husband I was just going to 'walk away' and headed to the end of what looked like a street. People were saying "No, no, don't go there, stay here!" When I got to the end of the shops I understood why. At the end of the street was a high fence and behind it were tiny hovels of homes in the dirt, with surprised people and children looking at me. I turned around to go look for my husband. "We have to leave," I told him. "We have to leave NOW." He still was not bothered by all the pushing, nudging and desperation the people there were beginning to show since we had not brought anything. I grabbed his arm and tried to tug him back to where we had left the taxi. Thank goodness there was one there, but I dared not get into it until I saw the sticker on the front. The driver was very sympathetic and could see that I was very upset. My husband thought I was over-reacting. I really didn't care—I just wanted to get back to the ship!

That evening, the ship couldn't leave on time because four passengers were missing. They finally showed up. Their story was that the taxi they had taken drove them high into the hills, to a relative's small T-shirt shop and held them there, refusing to leave until they had bought several shirts. Then they brought them back to the ship.

Sometimes it's smart to just stay on the boat.

THE BRITISH WHOOPSIES

You know, everywhere you go isn't usually all fairy-dust and Day-Glo. There are always the ickies—the surprises and the unexpected. They are usually the ones you remember long after the other stories have faded. My second husband was a helicopter pilot and he used to say some things were like piloting airplanes - long and boring, interrupted by moments of stark terror. Not that memories are filled with terror, just that some are ... well ... funky.

Take for instance a trip to Scotland one weekend that my family made with another couple and their daughter. We each drove our own cars. We meant to ask ahead for reservations but were assured by many of our British friends that reservations absolutely would not be necessary this time of year. Little did we or they know that a convention of ten thousand Jehovah Witnesses had booked Edinburgh, Scotland for the same time we would arrive. We were headed off into The Perfect Storm.

Once we understood our dilemma, we drove along the

eastern coast of Scotland, stopping at all possibilities, asking if they had rooms. We were fifty miles north when we finally found a pub that had two available rooms upstairs. The two older boys (twelve and ten) stretched out on two loveseats, trying to get comfortable. We made a bed somewhere for the two-year-old. My husband and I, at about 12 A.M. in the morning gratefully sank into the ¾ size bed. My side was wet.

Scotland is not that large. We easily spent the next day driving around the coasts, making stops to look for the Loch Ness Monster, meals and rest breaks before we thought it best to begin looking for a place to spend the night as we got closer to the Edinburgh area. Nothing … nothing … nothing. It finally became so late at night that we all opted to stop in a rest area and try to sleep in our cars for a while. I don't know what the others did, but in the back of our car, the boys laid the luggage as flat as they could in our Volkswagen square-back and tried to stretch out on top of it. My husband and I sat up front. It was hopeless. At daybreak, our friend tapped on a window and said, "Let's find a place for some breakfast."

The next place we saw was a truck-stop. The eight of us, cranky, cross and sleepy, stepped inside. There were a few truckers hunched over their mugs of coffee. It was dimly lit. The dirty counter had a big bowl of sugar and a large pitcher of cream on it. There was sugar and cream spilled everywhere. We got the kids some breakfasts and cups of coffee for ourselves. We stood there in silence, holding our coffees, taking in the counter, the mismatched chipped cups, flies buzzing, still feeling the shapes of the car armrests in our sides and I'm sure, all considering the trip so far.

My friend's wife looked at all of us and said after a moment, "A perfect end to a perfect day." I think if we hadn't looked dangerously unstable at that time, the owner might have asked us to leave because we couldn't stop laughing and crying.

British Leisure

Leisure is a great word. It implies so many ideas, most I could only have imagined in moments of escapism. Like those times of life when I felt as if small children were taped to the back of my knees most of the day or life was an overload of have-tos and need-tos that brought on those ethereal desires. Often, while staring out a window finishing up the dishes, the warm water and suds would lull me into a fantasy life. It's one in which someone else is doing the dishes while I'm dressing for another evening away and a motorcar with chauffeur will be driven up shortly, so I must hurry.

I had a mild approximation of that daydream for three years. A time of purely selfish devotion to myself, family, travel, ideas, new friends and exploration of a lovely country and lovely occupations. For the first time I had a housekeeper, gardener and a nanny on-call.

We had just moved to the Cotswold's of England, the 'garden spot' of Britain with truly all the gardens, thatched roofs, castles, and charm I could want. There were towns all around us with wonderful names, Chipping Camden, Bourton-on-the-Hill, Stow-on-the-Wold, Hinton-under-the-Hedge. We were three months in a hotel while waiting for our accommodations for the next three years to become available. What's not to like about that? Rooms cleaned, meals prepared, delightful conversations over a glass of sherry each evening in the hotel lounge with new friends before going into the dining room. All of that for a mom of three boys: two, ten and twelve, minus all the American lifestyle that went with working full time and a routine grown too familiar.

Once we settled into a home and began reaching out to the offerings of a lifetime, we began an English adventure to remember forever. Just getting to know the Americans and their excitement to be in their new and different homes and the English neighbors with their years of living in a land with different words, customs, ways of observing and relating was in itself satisfying and different.

As the boys settled into their routine of schools and activities and my husband began his association with his new surroundings, I was able to look around on my own and see what was available. It was a feast of opportunities. There must have been an activity club for every interest in town including quilting, needlepointing, painting, day trips to everything and place imaginable, a tea and pastry shop on every corner, towns full of antiques, trips to London for plays, musicals, personal sight-seeing, and unique places to eat and visit. Brass rubbings done in centuries old churches, festivals and fairs each weekend. It left me breathless and charmed! Dinners in castles using only a wooden spoon (I still have mine) and fish and chips or plough-man's lunches served everywhere.

The clubs and associations with the British and American women were wonderful and each out-did themselves in trying to be unique in their planned recreations for each other. One meeting might be listening to and identifying birdcalls, the women actually making the calls themselves. Another might feature a hypnotist or an incredible demonstration of some talent or collection. I was able to attend part-time for three years a Design College and made many train trips into London to galleries and museums with a like-minded friend who also was interested in designing needlepoints and painting.

I was able to make many gowns for all the social events we were to attend, finally having a chance to do as much sewing as I wanted. We did many things together with both American and British groups, some involving notables who would visit from the Embassy in London, to whom we were attached via our husband's workplaces. Color me happy! It was a gracious feeling to even pretend we had 'potential' possibilities for royal sightings. Since there was a racetrack in town, the Queen Mother was often there to be a part of it.

We weren't always self-absorbed. We, as a group attended nursing homes, made cookies, visited, sang to and played instruments for the residents. We also hosted visiting Americans in our homes. We filled in for moms in hospitals and helped out wherever we could with families. We planned and hosted the first American quilt show in that part of England. It was a huge affair, filling an enormous barn with personal quilts, many sent from the States.

One of my favorite things to do was to put my youngest son behind me on my bike, head downtown to a charming park and have lunch together there. It had wood and canvas sling chairs all around, ducks and swans on a lake, willows, a lunch canteen where I could buy lemonade and cucumber with butter sandwiches. We would spread a blanket out in some shade, and I would read a book to him. It was pure heaven.

I joined a small needlepointing group of women, that was taught by someone who had a 'title.' She was elderly and had decided to dedicate her life to teaching needlepoint. We would meet once a week in her beautiful back garden and were served pastries and cups of tea while she demonstrated the art of filling canvases with threads of wool. Her language was elite. She and her poise were elegant as she explained the intricate patterns of needlepointing or petite pas, as she called it. Each week as we entered her home, she would have mounds of examples or unfinished pieces she was working with, on a center table in the hall for us to examine and talk about.

Occasionally, a group of women would make trips into the small towns to look through antiques. Often, many of them were marked 'sold' and were being shipped to the States. It was rumored that Jacqueline Kennedy was always in that part of the area also shopping. We never did catch up with her.

I made many delightful friends among the British neighbors and people that I met in England. One has been a penpal for 44 years. I just heard from her last week. She led me down the path of doll houses and treasures to fill them. I'm sad to admit that the unfinished dollhouse is still with me as are boxes of collections to fill it. Now, we chat about our children, her youngest was the age of my youngest, and now the grand and great-grandchildren over the years and we remember the wonderful memories of my fairy tale life while living there.

Probably the biggest leisure I had then was being able to spend as much time as I did with my family. We camped, spent time in other countries, drove all over Scotland, Wales, France, Italy and Germany. I love that we were able to have had those experiences together. I could only wish to do it all over again!

England—The Beginning Of A Three-Year Adventure

Five of us, an eighteen-month-old, ten-year-old and twelve-year-old boys, my husband and I are sitting in a lounge at the Baltimore airport, waiting to catch our flight to London, England. There is a woman, about fifty, staring intently at my husband. She gets up finally, comes over and says that she would like to 'paint' my husband. I recognize her as an internationally known artist, but she doesn't introduce herself. We are already deep into major frustration, excitement and exhaustion caused by preparing for the move, and are feeling the stiff anticipation of the decision we have made to move to another country. We can only look at her and say plainly what our circumstances are at the moment and feel an amazement that this would happen on this day. She looks oddly disappointed and says, "He has such an interesting face. When will you be back?"

"Three years," was my response. That pretty much ended the conversation.

I took different looks at my husband after that. He did have sort of a 'universal' face. Sometimes he reminded me of Omar Sharif. Other times, Elvis Presley. But mostly, he was the Tennessee boy I had known since the eighth grade.

At the moment I had an issue regarding a liter of wine I had been forced to add to my load of travel equipment and baby conveniences. A friend had come to see us off at the airport and thrust this thing at me, declaring in her excitement that we were to drink it in our new home. My husband, apparently charmed by the gesture, but not enough to carry the thing, dismissed my idea to give it away to some lucky worker and insisted that we carry it with us. Little did he know or remember whether we had it with us during the hubbub of arriving at London's Heathrow Airport because actually I had ditched it in the lady's room before departing Baltimore. I wasn't going to add that bottle to my already overloaded self and hoped that some lucky person would be happy to find it sitting there.

The flight was amazingly smooth and untroubled in spite of having been given a seat at the back of the plane where someone had thrown up onto my tray during the previous flight (the flight attendant did clean it as best she could, but it didn't do much for the aroma). My boys were happy to sit down and be quiet for a few hours and the baby slept most of the way until preparing for landing when his eardrums must have felt like they were going to implode. His screaming blended in with the other small children who were also screaming. A shrieking in many scales of musical notes, stopping and starting all over the plane like a merry-go-round calliope going off its rails.

My overwhelming first impression of being in England was

the smell of mothballs. It was May and London was having a serious cold snap. The Britishers had been forced to reclaim their winter-wear from storage which obviously included the use of mothballs. We were freezing in our Maryland spring outfits going through the airport, but the only thing on our minds was to claim our luggage, keep ourselves together and find the driver who had been sent by our new employers to drive us to our new home, Cheltenham, in Gloucestershire.

He was known throughout the British-American community as 'John, the Driver.' He was Santa-plump, ruddy-rosy, with a pork-pie hat, and able to move us along quickly, ever helpful, chatting away in what seemed at the time another language. He arranged us in the van, turned the heat up to sweltering and took off like the jolly madman he turned out to be. Between the exhaustion, motion, and heat we were all soon asleep as John got onto the motorway. At some point both my husband I woke up and slowly leaned forward to look at the speedometer. He was cruising and weaving in and out at 104 mph. We whispered "John, you are going pretty fast."

"Oh, it's OK," he replied. "Never any trouble along here, but I'll slow down a bit if you like." We liked. I don't think he was very happy about the slow-down because it was an American supplied car, and he felt permission to do as he wished by virtue of the exalted position driving the car afforded him. We learned later that he indeed had a personal mission to set records for how fast he could get new personnel from the London airport to Cheltenham. We had messed with his goals.

John dropped us off in front of what turned out to be our new home for the next three months. A lovely, three story hotel ran by Mr. and Mrs. Weaver. Everything to our American eyes was charming and British, but at the moment, overwhelming. Stimulus was coming from every direction and every sound. My three boys were flexing their muscles up for big leaps forward, having sat for the past ten hours in airports, planes and cars.

We were shown to our rooms on the second floor, vaguely registering the entire differences to what we had known all out lives, with the huge spaciousness, walls lined with potted plants, shelves of books, heavy draperies, large windows, antique-looking paintings and portraits. "Come down when you are ready, and we will show you around," was a cheery offer from the owner. Now that I think of it, Mr. Weaver reminded me of James Harriot's brother, Charles, in the *All Creatures Great and Small* TV series: a capable, comfortable, fiftyish man always in a shirt, tie, sweater vest and tweed jacket and able to move more quickly than I thought possible.

We showed up for a look around, which included a lounge where the only TV was, which we discovered, showed mostly horse-racing and messages from the Queen during the day. The lounge was filled with overstuffed mis-matched and multi-floral furniture, a tight, wood-paneled dining room for breakfasts, dinner teas, and an ever-present electric kettle, teapot, cups, milk and sugar. Biscuits, cookies to us, were provided in the evenings. We asked directions to the nearest shopping area. We needed sweaters! We were freezing, not prepared for the cold weather. There were no 'shopping centers' as such. We would need to catch a bus downtown.

What a dizzying day! There were language barriers, sounds that made no sense, all new architecture, car differences, many lovely things to look at, and liking and wondering at every-thing we saw. There was a problem in asking questions because we used the wrong words, as in 'drug store' being a chemist or pharmacy, along with stores having nicknames and of course the money differences. We were forever discussing the color, shape and weight of coins.

The oldest boys were soon enrolled in a local school run by monks. I have no good explanation for doing that other than perhaps I thought it would be a good experience for them. The regular British school, more like the U.S. version, did not have as good a reputation, and the only other choice was the U.S. school for elementary children, an hour's bus trip to a military installation and back each day. No … monk's school it was. There was a very posh and expensive boarding school that was available and an American family near us did send their boys there to board even though the school was only a few blocks from their home. I never figured that out, even though the par-ents were loving, and their boys seemed to me to be kind and well-behaved. Translation: Not that much trouble at home, why board them away for the week?

We had to shop for short gray pants, gray shirts and ties, gray cap and gray jumper sweaters and jackets with the school's emblem on it. The boys only had a few weeks of school left, so off they went each morning. The conversations when they returned were quiet and accusatory. They didn't like the short pants. Apparently, lunches were alien and odd but they loved them. There were banged-up metal pots of tea on the tables. The tea was always strong, sweetened with condensed milk. Cornish pasties were served once per week, and they couldn't get enough of those, stuffing their pockets with them. Mutton, shepherd's pie, bangers and mash (sausages and potatoes), and pork pies were other male food delights. Dessert always included gallons of custard. Adkins diet reigned supreme and included everything a health-conscious mother avoided.

We lived in the hotel for three months while looking for and ultimately waiting for rental openings to become available, as we were one of the last American families to arrive. I have to say, not having to clean, cook or provide entertainment for those months was delightful and not unnoticed. There was another family there also waiting for accommodations, but more about them later. They had been to Cheltenham before and knew to hold out for something spectacular to live in for three years. I wish we had been as knowledgeable and savvy. I just wanted to get my family into anything that was big enough.

What we found was a semi-detached rental. Duplex to Americans, but with an air space between the two buildings for noise proofing. For our neighbor's sakes, I hope to heavens it worked.

While we were in the hotel, the boys had a room to themselves and my husband and I shared ours with our 18-month-old son. We had only one tall wardrobe for our clothes and Adam, our son, had a small dresser to himself.

Within a couple of months, Adam began showing small, odd marks along his shoulders. They ran in a straight line with eruptions at regular intervals. When they began appearing along his arms we made an appointment with a local doctor, which was not easy to do since England used socialized medicine and one is usually 'assigned' to the doctor in our area that required waiting a long time to be seen. Because we were 'paying customers', we moved to the top of the list. The doctor, who was impeccably dressed, had a lovely office with medical journals inside beautiful cases, plants, and draperies. He sat across from us behind his magnificent desk and said, "I have never seen anything like this before." By that time the marks on his little body were everywhere, straight lines and eruptions, and he was covered with encrusted sores making him cranky and feverish. We saw two more physicians over the course of two weeks, both who seemed to be puzzled by what they could see, but no diagnosis.

After much agonizing and conversations with our fellow Americans with children, we decided to make a trip to the nearest American military base to let the pediatrician there have a look at him.

We were anxious and preoccupied as we made the hour drive through the countryside to the base, Adam finally fell peacefully asleep in the back seat.

We were ushered into the examining room and told to remove everything on Adam except his diaper. He was quietly sitting on the table when the doctor walked in, drying his hands on paper towels, and said, "Oh my god. Look at that. The kid's got scabies."

Now, I don't wish to malign anyone or practice medicine without a license, but of all the places in the world I thought might recognize a case of scabies, it would have been England. Didn't all those sailors on the old ships have them?

We were instructed to wash all of his clothes in boiling water and put a special cream on his entire body three times a day for twenty minutes and then wash it off. We did that for two weeks. The scabies disappeared. Later they reappeared around his waist. In the boiling of the clothes, I decided not to boil his little belt since it was elastic. Scabies were in the belt. For some reason, I remember the last treatment better than the first because he had been through the first two weeks and neither of us were happy about doing it for two more weeks! Even a baby can harbor a considerable amount of hostility, given the right circumstances.

An aside to British medical assignments, we were assigned to the local doctor when we moved to a permanent residence. My husband fell and had a possible broken wrist. The doctor we met seemed to be more interested in talking about the huge refrigerators and washer/dryers the Americans had brought with them than my husband's problem. When he did focus on the patient, he grabbed my husband's wrist and twisted it, asking, "Does that hurt?" My husband turned white and dropped to the floor on his knees. Doctor Looney-tunes said, "It's not broken," and put a wrapper around it. We did decide that we hereafter would take our medical needs to the nearest military base. When we gently asked our British neighbors about their visits to the doctor, they responded, "Oh ... do you mean the sadist?"

Lucky us.

Two other episodes caused us to question the treatment of children. Adam had his finger smashed in a car door, and it looked to be hanging by a strip of skin. We drove him to the local hospital. The nurse took him away after diagnosing for treatment. I think he could have been heard screaming blocks away. They sewed his finger back together without numbing it.

We asked about that and were told they never used numbing solutions because at that age they were too young to feel pain. Later, our oldest son had to have two teeth extracted due to dental crowding. Apparently, the dentists didn't subscribe to a numbing procedure either. We picked up our thirteen-year-old who was almost passing out and white. His level of trust in both his parents and dentists was not high that day and for a long time afterward.

These are some of the beginning adventures we had during the three years of living a fairy tale life in a country filled with amazing beauty and people.

Moving Parts

In three words I can
sum up everything
I've learned in life:
it goes on.
Robert Frost

OAK RIDGE, TENNESSEE: THE SECRET CITY

The houses are what I remember first. They were lined up and down all the streets, exactly alike, square and gray little flat-topped boxes, one beside the other. Hundreds of them, with long boardwalks built across and on top of the red clay to access the street and cars, which were parked on the gravel road, and to reach the coal bins at the end of the boardwalks. There was a character to them, simply in the number of them and their sameness. Standing alone, one would have looked forgotten and odd, unfinished, but together they looked significant.

The year was 1943. Oak Ridge (un-named at the time) was to be a secret city. It would participate in the creation of the atomic bomb that would ultimately end World War Two.

Consider the planning, construction, and operation of a military reservation. As an example, say that someone would contact a Holiday Inn company and ask them to buy up sixty acres in the foothills of Eastern Tennessee. In six months' time:

have land and utilities installed; build homes in eight months for twenty thousand families that would be arriving there; also provide restaurants, schools, water, electricity, transportation, a hospital and a local newspaper. The population would increase to seventy-five thousand in one and a half years and would be fed, housed, educated and transported to and from work and NO ONE IS TO KNOW ABOUT IT!

The area chosen was Black Oak Ridge. It already had rail lines, was a safe distance from the coast, had high ridges to muffle possible explosions and contamination and hide the working plants from saboteurs, and dams for electricity. It was perfect.

The land was cleared of trees and bushes in one day, leaving the red-clay mud exposed. The next day the trucks started rolling in with the modules. The third day, there were houses on stilts in the area. This is according to someone who was interviewed years later.

The square box houses were prefabricated of a new material, called Cemesto. It was created by rolling cement and asbestos together into panels, and the houses came in three sections. The local roads were choked for months when the trucks began bringing the modules for installation. Most had a living/dining room area dominated by a pot-bellied coal stove, a kitchen, a bathroom with a tiny shower. On the other side, two bedrooms separated by a small walk-in closet with shelving where my mother kept the washing machine that had to be rolled into the kitchen for use. The very basic of needs for a family of five. I do remember that the flooring at the time were sheets of Masonite screwed down and showed every stain, much to my mother's dismay. Rugs were an immediate necessity for warmth and appearance. These buildings were called square, matchbox demountables.

The population would be 75,000 with 10,000 more dwelling units eventually. The houses would be near a work area one and one-half miles wide and six and a half miles long. Workers were recruited from all over the nation and NOT told what they were going to be doing. Staff were brought in to design the community centers, banks, schools, post office, bus terminals, clothing stores, 10-cent stores, movie theaters, supermarkets, bowling alleys and football fields. The area of Oak Ridge was not shown on any maps until after the war was over.

Children grew up in the shadow of the world's most secretive undertaking, "behind a fence". A diverse population with varied socio-economic levels. The community was youthful, and ages ranged from thirty to forty years old. The highest birth rate in the nation was there. No class distinctions were made, although the Negro families were segregated. Education was progressive or modern. I remember Helen Keller and her dog coming to visit our school. No one was allowed to own property, but only rent for $30 to $85 a month. Because it was a military reservation, parents had little reason to fear for the safety of children. We were never afraid and had great freedom to roam the hills. Children ten years or older also had passes, along with their parents, to get in or out of the reservation that had triple fences armed by patrols and guard towers.

Behind our house were woods covering a hill which was a great discovery because we had never seen anything like them in the flat land of Venice, California. And roam we did. We found a stream at the bottom of the hill and blackberry bushes. We saw foxes and played hide and seek in the trees. We caught June bugs, tied a length of thread around their little bodies and instantly had our own tiny flying kites. Because of the dirt and mud, my mother tethered my two-year-old brother to the large oak beside the boardwalk, each morning, so he would have a clean place to play on the boardwalk and be in the shade. I remember one day thinking how empty and plain the front yard was, so I systematically planted acorns everywhere, imagining the grove we would have to play in.

On one side of us was a family who seemed to live differently than mine did. I think their father must have been one of the engineers. The boy and girl were always neat and pressed. Her hair was always curled and in ribbons. He wore a little belt with his shorts. They never went barefoot - something to which we were quickly becoming fond of, especially since the red-clay mud ruined our shoes. They introduced themselves by all three of their names - first, middle and last. Looking back, I can only think their mother must have thought we were urchins. I peeked through their screened door once to see their table set for lunch: placemats, silverware, napkins and glasses of iced tea with lemon slices. I was mesmerized. We usually had a dish, a paper napkin and a sandwich that we picked up from the kitchen. Ours was a communal effort. Their children seemed to be waited on by their parents. A new look at another life.

The size and type of the homes were given by family size. There were 4 theaters, 6 recreation halls, bowling alleys, twenty-three tennis courts, swimming pool, ball parks, taverns and a 9,400-volume library. There was a little theater, music society, concerts, community sings. All free. For a fee, one could use the skating rink, amusement parks, and art school. There was an openness to religion—Methodists and Baptists shared the same building. Among the Jews, Catholics and Protestants, there was cooperation and understanding. There was something called The Group Insurance Plan that cost $4 per family a month and included children under nineteen years. There was no private practice, but the doctors made house calls. The hospital had 300 beds. There were five psychiatrists and they practiced group therapy. Many families were lured by the high wages to make their way to Oak Ridge.

Most of these amenities and social understandings didn't exist in the little town we moved to after the war was over. And it was only fifteen miles away. Gone was the pool, little theater, concerts, art school, amusement park and movie theaters. Enter: division and segregation of people and religions in a small community in a southern town.

Dad's Farm

After living in Oak Ridge, Tennessee during the war years, my parents decided to move to a small town fifteen miles away. My dad would still be working at one of the plants at the Atomic Energy facility.

My parents were just fortunate enough to have had a financial windfall at that time, so Dad bought Mother a fur coat and a home sitting on seven acres. I remember going to seeing the property the first time when they were considering buying it. Even I could see the house was going to require a lot of remodeling and cosmetic changes. The sale included a garage at the bottom of our hill. It must have been a small business at one time for car repairs, changing oil or whatever care a car might need. Dad was ecstatic and proud that there was an oil-changing bay which he could simply drive his car over to change his own oil. Mother said that was why he wanted the property.

I think the first farm animals Dad invested in were a pair of bantam chickens with lovely feathers on their legs. They were friendly enough that Dad thought to bring them into the house a time or two to try taming them. He got as far as one chicken sitting with him in his chair, but I guess the excitement was too much for the chicken and it did a whoopsie down his shirt as he was petting it. That was the end of his chicken experiment. Next was a goat that someone gave him. He tied him to a tree in the back to 'let it get used to being around there.' The first time he was untied, the goat leaped in about 3 bounds down our hill, across the road and down the neighbors hill before disappearing out of sight.

Next was a piglet whom Mother named "Joseph." Dad thought it would be safer in a proper sty, which was in back. Joe, as he became known, was very friendly. He grew fast that summer. He was allowed out of his pen and came down to hang out with the three of us. He loved to be squirted with the hose. Joe was very smart, and he watched us take turns getting in and out of a hammock Dad had put up. As we sat at dinner one night, we saw him put his front legs in the hammock and walk and back and forth making it 'swing.' In the meantime, Mom and Dad had quietly bought a freezer chest. We all saw it, but no one said anything about it. Joe finally had grown enough that my brother was able to sit on his back. Joe was big enough now to "take a ride" in a neighbor's truck. We all knew what Joe was being raised for but did not acknowledge it. Dad returned with a carload of wrapped packages. He said that Joe had sustained a badly sprained leg and could not be slaughtered, and that the packages "contained another pig given in substitution."

It didn't work. We were all silent for days, miserable, not wanting to go near the freezer chest. We all knew that was Joe in there. My poor parents finally gave up and gave everything away, the freezer, its contents, their good intentions and dreams of animal husbandry ... and took up gardening.

Dad did find success in one thing—bee keeping. He took to it like a Bee Charmer and bought all the things he needed: hives, trays of wax, and a 'smoker' to make them sleepy when he needed to clean the hives or harvest some honey ... and bees. He was able to collect a swarm that a friend notified him was in a nearby tree. He put on his hat with the veil, long sleeves, gloves, got his smoker and took off, returning with the clump of bees on a limb. Somehow, he got them into one of the hives and harvested honey for years.

One thing my parents tried that did not work out well was 'tanning' a hide. They got the idea when they found a raccoon alongside a highway and brought it home to skin. My sister and I were full of reasons and advice as to how to get rid of it and why. But their decision had been made, and they were prepared to experiment. The odor was indescribable. What they were doing was out of science fiction or a horror movie, as far as we were concerned. Who WERE these people?! Our brother was delighted and watched the whole thing. They tacked the skin to the back of the smoke house and left it to cure. It simply smelled bad and disintegrated, little by little. We avoided going back there for weeks. I now wonder what they thought they would do with it if the adventure had been successful. A floor rug? Hang it on a wall? A small coat?

The last animal episode I remember was ... the turkey. My parents had bought it for Thanksgiving dinner. He was tethered outside for a few days. We discovered quickly that he didn't like anyone going near him. My sister and I did not like speculating on what would to happen to him.

The day before Thanksgiving arrived. Mother was not feeling well, and Dad had to work overtime, so he was not going to be able to prepare the offering for our feast ahead of time. So help me, Mother sent us outside with an ax to begin the preparations. She said, "Just cut off the head. I'll take care of the rest of it." I think my sister was eight and I was eleven. WHAT made her think that was a reasonable thing to do? Two kids with an ax and a very nervous turkey. A BIG turkey.

Ok. Mom seemed to think we could do it. It was cold outside. We wanted to get it over with. We looked at the bird, talked about how and who would do what. I picked up the ax. The thing was heavy! Our idea was that we would catch the turkey, she would hold the turkey's neck over a rather large stump in the back yard and I would whack it. I don't remember actually catching the turkey, which was still tied up, but somehow, we caught it and my sister had its neck stretched over the stump. I raised the ax and brought it down. Not too bad for a couple of novices, but the cut had not gone all the way through, and the poor bird's neck was dangling. It was thrashing around, and we couldn't get hold of it again. Mom, who had been watching, said to just come in the house and that we had done our best. I don't think she was looking forward to plucking it anyway.

Like the great holiday movie, The Christmas Story, that was the beginning of our yearly trip into Knoxville each Thanksgiving to have our dinner at a Chinese restaurant. I don't think any of us wanted any reminders of the Great Thanksgiving Day Turkey Massacre.

BACK ON THE FARM
(A FIVE ACT PLAY)

SCENE 1: *Diane and Loretta are looking at a crate that has two chickens in it.*

Loretta: "What are those?"

Diane: "Bantam chickens, I think."

Loretta: "Hmmm. Why does Dad have them?"

Diane: "I don't know. Someone gave them to him."

SCENE 2: *Diane and Loretta are walking towards the living room and see Dad with one of the chickens.*

Loretta: " Why is the chicken in the house?"

Diane: " I don't know. Maybe he wants it to sit with him."

They stand and watch as Dad puts the chicken on his chest. The chicken does a 'whoopsie' on his shirt.

Diane: "That's not good."

SCENE 3: *A small piglet is being uncrated outside by Dad as Diane, Loretta and Mom watch.*

Mom: "This is Joseph. He's going to live in the pig sty on the hill, in back."

Loretta: "He's so cute! He's pink and has a little curly tail!"

Mom: "Now, he's not to play with. We're just going to let him grow to be a big boy."

Dad puts the pig on the ground and everyone beams.

Mom: "Remember, Joseph has to stay in his pen."

Diane and Loretta: (under their breaths) "Yeah, right."

Six months later. Joseph weighs about two hundred pounds. A new freezer is sitting in the laundry room.

Dad: " Joseph has a bad leg. I need to put him in the truck and take him to the vet and have it checked."

Everyone watches as the truck drives away with Joseph in the back of it.

Diane: (Looking at Loretta) "This doesn't look good."

Dad returns with packages wrapped in white freezer paper.

Dad: "The vet had to keep Joseph because of his bad leg. This is another pig."

Dad puts the packages in the freezer. Everyone knows that's Joe in there. Mom and Dad give the freezer and contents away.

SCENE 4: *Diane and Loretta are outside.*

Loretta: "Phew! What's that smell?!"

Diane: "I don't know!"

They walk up to Mom and Dad who are working with something on a table.

Diane: "Oh, that doesn't look good!"

Loretta: "What's that?!"

Dad: "We found it by the road. We're going to skin and tan the hide to see what happens."

Diane: "That doesn't sound good"!

Loretta: "Where are you going to put it?"

Mom: "We're going to nail it on the side of the smoke house until it dries."

Loretta: "What is it?"

Mom: "A raccoon."

Diane: "That's not gonna be good!"

Loretta: "What will it be?"

Mom: "We'll see after it dries."

Show the hide on the side of the smokehouse as the sun, rain, and wind blows it away. Only the nails are finally left.

Diane: "That's good."

SCENE 5: *Thanksgiving Day. A turkey is tied up in the back yard. Mom and the two girls, 10 and 7, are in the kitchen.*

Mom: "I've got a little job for you two girls."

Diane: "What's that, Mom?"

Mom: "I need you to cut the head off the turkey."

Loretta: "That's not good."

Backyard: The two girls with an axe are looking at the turkey.

Diane: "I guess you could hold his neck on the stump and I could whack it with the axe."

Loretta: "Mom seems to think we can do this."

Next scene: *Dad arrives to see his two girls with a turkey whose head is dangling from its neck.*

Dad: "That's never good."

Mom: "It's OK. You girls did your best."

EXIT SCENE: *Everyone is in the car, heading west, for Thanksgiving Day dinner in Knoxville.*

THE END

ACROSS THE HIGHWAY

It started with a notice from a high school friend that a mutual classmate had passed away. There began a trickle of memories, which became a stream of old recollections.

We had moved to our home in Kingston, Tennessee in the late 1940s. We had originally lived in Oak Ridge, Tennessee, during the war years and my Californian parents, liking the area, decided to stay in the small foothills of the Smoky Mountains. They found a house three miles from the town. At that time, it felt as if we were out in the country. The house was perfect for us, although it needed a great deal of remodeling and attention. It was built on a small bluff, sitting alongside and above Highway 70. There was a separate garage at the bottom of the hill, which I'm sure figured in an important way to my dad in his decision to buy the seven and a half acres. Mother would have plenty of spaces, finally, to plant flowers after living with the sterile, clay soil of Oak Ridge.

One, among many of the good features, was a small, one room grocery store with a single gas pump, located right across the road from us. The fact the owners lived nearby and had eleven children was exciting. We would have a great selection of friends and playmates built right in!

I recently looked at an obituary announcement with the listing of family names and was saddened to read that only the two youngest girls were still around. They were probably the two we were closest to, because they were near my sister's and my age when we moved there. We were in the fourth and second grades then. How emotional it felt to read nine of their names, as now being gone. The two youngest girls who had been our school friends, were the only ones still living. The names of the two parents were shown to be Ernest and Sophia, something I never knew, because we only called them Mr. and Mrs. Pierce. From that distance in time and filtered through memories, Sophia now seems very exotic for that time period.

I don't know which family extended the first invitation to visit, but I remember many games of hopscotch, jacks and jumping rope, usually out under a cluster of trees. Their home had the most abundant table of goodies I had ever seen in my life. There were always platters and bowels of good things to eat sitting around, with gauzy covers over them to keep any insects away. My attention was always towards the three and four-layer cakes that Mrs. Pierce made, along with many pies and biscuits, usually sitting together. She was very generous with her slices of goodies.

She and my mother became good friends, often visiting across the highway. One of my surprises was that Mrs. Pierce dipped snuff and always had an empty coffee can near her chair to spit in. I'd never seen a woman do that but discovered it to be an old-time route to nicotine addiction. She was eternally knitting or crocheting some item. It was often a doily for the back of the chairs or some pieces to display on the arms of the furniture. There were also large, beautiful lacy ones she had made for her tables. She may have been the one who taught me to crochet. Mrs. Pierce was the first person I knew to pass away. I could never forget the sadness and weeping of her large family.

The brother, Alvin, was my secret sweetheart, even though he was about fifteen years old to my ten. The father often supplemented his income by driving to Detroit with one or more of his sons to pick up used cars to sell on the lot, in front of his store. There even was a large cage with a monkey in it, out in front of the store for a time, as a tourist attraction. The store was one of the few businesses in eastern Tennessee, in those years, that would allow Negroes to use their restroom.

At some point, Mr. and Mrs. Pierce decided to build a new home. They moved all of their furnishings to the basement of the grocery store during the entire time the building was going on, and they all lived in that tight closeness. My sister and I were often invited to spend the night with the two youngest girls in their new spaces and loved all the differences it made. When someone had that many children, I guess two more weren't going to make a big difference. The house, when finished, was larger than the original and very nice. Mrs. Pierce and her family of helpers kept it gleaming and neat.

Mrs. Pierce was a woman with many skills, coping with such a large family. One day, I had stepped on a nail. I began to see a red line going up my leg. I had always heard that if that happened and it got to your heart, you would die! My parents had gone to Knoxville that morning to do some shopping, when I decided that I definitely needed to talk to Mrs. Pierce about the problem. She took a look at it, got out a small metal pan, some wool and matches. She made a small fire with the wool in the pan, to create smoke. She then held the smoking pan under my foot. I am here today to declare that we watched that red line slowly move down my leg like reading a thermometer until it disappeared. I asked her how that happened, and she said she didn't know, but it just always worked. She had lots of those home remedies.

All of us girls rode school buses together for our elementary school years, and I guess it was when we entered high school that we began to go different ways when dating began. It's surprising to think that all of those years spent together ended without out being in touch. I think it's probably because we moved away and they mostly stayed within the area, marrying classmates or friends. I have a satellite picture of the entire area that shows the current owners of my parent's property had the entire acreage cleared and the house and garage torn down.

Also shown in that satellite picture is the small store and house, still across the highway.

From Another Galaxy

Fourth grade was my personal introduction into the mores of the South. Each day I observed changes subtle and not so subtle by simply being among my classmates. Language barriers were the first to sort out. My new southern friends made different sounds than I did. Cain't, ain't, hain't, awl (for oil). They talked with a slower rhythm and somehow managed to add several syllables to a one-syllable word.

They all knew each other like a big family, and they nosed up like friendly pups to check you out. The first issue was "Which side are you on?" I had no idea what they were talking about. "You know," they said, "which side of the Silver War are you on?"

I had never heard of this war. When I asked my dad when I got home, which side of this I was supposed to be on, he said, "Just tell them you're from California." That was perfect. That's all they wanted to know. The question never came up again, but I sensed a subtle change in my position among my peers. I was a foreigner.

One of my new friends eventually asked me to ride home on her bus and spend the night. My parents encouraged me to meet new friends, so away I went to what seemed to be Never-never Land. They had no indoor plumbing other than a hand-cranked water pump in the kitchen. That meant using a back house outside for bathroom needs. Not good in the dark. We roamed through freshly plowed fields while she told me what had been planted, and she knew all the little green sprouts. Her mother was kind but busy, having to care for a new baby. To rock the baby to sleep, she had a straight-legged wooden chair, outside on a porch, in which she sat with the baby cradled to her shoulder and rocked violently back and forth, the wooden legs slamming loudly on the porch. That child was asleep in no time. From this point in time I now wonder. Was it a mild form of shaken baby syndrome being used as a sleeping aid?

Those were the school days when all subjects were taught in the same room. We only left it for lunch, or recesses or special programs, until we graduated from eighth grade. I loved the lunches, which were only 35 cents. They often had white whipped potatoes each week, and a dessert. I don't remember any of the desserts, but the potatoes were a marvel of fluffy goodness. Mother's style always had lumps, which I remember affectionately whenever I now run across some in a meal.

I was with that group of people for nine years of my life. We grew from children to young adults together, with all the angsts that go with it. We were like a large group of cousins, knowing where all the buttons where and how to administer goodness or mischief towards each other. Whenever we now meet at reunions, I am always amazed at the unique ability to be seventeen or eighteen years old again, if only for a few hours, because that's how we knew each other last.

Distances of
Time and Place

I have a black-and-white picture of a young family. They are standing in front of a fence with a billboard, stores, a street off in the distance, behind them. The sun might have been causing a glare because they are all squinting or lowering their heads. The dad is holding a young, curly-haired blond boy, the wife is beside him and two small girls are standing in front of them. They have a 'look' about them. I have often wondered what that 'look' was. Anticipation? There is an energy to it. This seems an important moment to them. There are other pictures with this one family grouping—the girls standing beside a bicycle, the boy alone by the fence. Another, of the mother standing behind the boy with one hand on his shoulder. I would say that they are all dressed for the occasion—the mother wearing a two-piece dress with a clasp of jewelry on her shoulder, the dark lipstick of the era, which I would guess to be in the 40s, the girls in similar dresses—short puffed sleeves and sashes, short white stockings with their white buckled shoes.

The boy has a long-sleeved shirt and what looks to be corduroy overalls with the straps crossed in the back and buttoned in the front. The father is dressed in obvious khaki pants and shirt. Possibly a holdover from recently leaving the military?

I found out years later that this indeed was an important picture, an important moment. The father was leaving his family in Venice, California that day to travel to a new opportunity in Oak Ridge, Tennessee. The family would join him later. He had been hired as an electrician, to be part of the ultra-secret Manhattan Project in development there. No one knew what was being built behind the fenced, armed-guarded areas there, only that the wages were good, rentals were provided for a small amount and most facilities for the families were excellent, innovative and free ... and travel was paid for, by the government.

We, as children, were not aware of the plans our parents were making for us. Only that we would be moving soon. We continued our lives as before with the help of relatives. I still took my dimes to school to be put into cards with little slots to hold them, 'for the war effort'. We, as children, had no notion of what was going on in the world. We couldn't know about the battles being fought on the other side of the world, trying to keep Japan and Germany from dominating others ... what our father and other fathers would be working on that would help create an atomic bomb that would change the world forever. We did know how to do the name-calling epitaphs of Tojo, Mussolini and Hitler when we wanted to give a bad label someone. So, some of the essence of the day did manage to seep down into the behavior of the children.

How brave our parents were, to leave all they knew, travel across the country yet again, to work and live in an area, about which, they could be told nothing. I wonder what they talked about in discussing this with others and themselves. I remember that they seemed to be happy with the circumstances there. And there was a great sense of 'community' among the neighbors. My parents kept those same people they met in Oak Ridge, Tennessee, as close friends their whole lives, later living a few miles from each other, when they bought homes in the area after the war was over.

I wonder now what all that newness of other people brought to the area. People from all over the world, working for a common good and then spreading out into the surrounding communities. Communities that had been established here for generations, and now they had to adjust to folks who had not considered their personal history of Civil War, slavery, or southern ideas. I only thought of how I experienced the friends I knew, but I seldom thought about what they had to come to terms with, regarding the people now moving and living amongst them. What were their evaluations of us?

I had heard my fourth-grade school friends whisper to me, my first day of school, "Which side of the Silver War are you on?" I couldn't answer this, never having heard of the Silver War. I asked my dad for an answer when I returned home, and he said, "Just tell them that you are from California." Which was the perfect answer ... but I was now a considered a foreigner.

I can attest to the fact that those circumstances didn't change over the years. There was always a separation, however slight, among my school friends and myself, and as far I as could tell, between my parents and the local people. They still chose their war years friends, who were from all over the states, over the nearest neighbors. The Tennesseans were kind and friendly but didn't necessarily associate with the strangers filtering out into their established areas. The strangers were kindly 'tolerated.'

There were already behaviors and objections in place, such as how they felt about living with and tolerating the Negro people, Catholics and Jewish people living in the area. Catholics were whispered about and quietly identified. I remember being puzzled over the objections they had about the young Catholic girls having pierced ears. This was considered wanton and sinful in those days. But then, I myself was an object of consideration when I wore sleeveless dresses or tops. The Blacks were the most ill-treated of all. In the '40s, they were expected to step off the sidewalk when white people passed.

Seen talking to them was risky and could cause the Ku Klux Klan to burn a cross on your front lawn that night. I saw many of those cross-shaped burned spots from my school bus and then would miss seeing those friends whose families usually quietly left town.

My mother was an accepting Californian, and just treated everyone the same. She made it a point to speak to everyone and make friends with everyone. The Black people began waiting for her on the corners in town because they knew she was always going to stop and chat with them and ask about their families. I could see by the looks on their faces, that they liked her and waited for her to catch up with them. I think she was able to get away with this without anyone rebuking her or burning anything on our lawns because she had an obvious handicap and used it to her advantage. She was pretty sure no one wanted to be accused of harassing someone who had difficulty in walking and had spastic limbs simply because she stopped to speak to people, regardless of their color. Mother was a very smart woman and knew how to use some things to her advantage. And she simply loved people, most of all, when they were needy, misunderstood and especially when they were brave and standing up for the respect they deserved.

I haven't returned to that town too many times, over the years. Nothing has made me want to go back very often, other than curiosity. It's still the same 'steeped in tradition' spot that it always was. The biggest source of friendships were always the people in my school classes. Since I didn't have many relatives, they always felt like my big family of cousins with all their opinions, issues and caring. I love being with them now, as gray and white-haired adults together - we have all softened, having been through our fiery trials, and can now appreciate that we indeed, are an accepting family that did and do care for each other.

ROUTE 2

I received a call from my sister last year; she seemed a little dazed and confused. "It's not there," she began, "it's all gone. I feel like I'm standing in another country."

"What do you mean?" I asked. "What's going on?"

She answered, "I'm standing across the street from where we used to live, and I can't make any sense of it. The entire property is scraped clean. There's no house, no garage, no driveway, no nothing. Just a hill of grass."

I asked, "What else is around you?" She said, "Just the usual houses still across the street, but everything on our side is gone."

How strange it all sounded. I had the immediate feeling 'shouldn't someone have been notified?' Never mind that the property had been sold and re-sold multiple times. At the moment, it just seemed as if it was important that the ones to whom the land probably meant the most, should have been warned or been told that the entire property was going to be obliterated. That's not exactly a rational thought, but, some-where inside on an emotional level, it made sense.

One of my sons sent me the satellite view of the site, and it did indeed show that there was nothing left. Even the trees up the hill, behind the house, had been cleared. I stared at the picture a long time, trying to put it into a familiar focus of some kind. I had to remember that when my parents bought the house and property in 1948, the house was probably fifteen years old, so the building had been very close to eighty-five years old when removed.

But it is still strange to see everything wiped out, as if they had never existed.

Since then, I have been aware of my memories fleshing out the years of the house and the area, putting them together, getting them in order. Many years had been spent there.

The property with the house, a separate working garage and pump house, were three and a half miles from the nearest town of Kingston, Tennessee. That's not very far, distance-wise, but it felt as though we were miles out in the country with few homes at that time since we had been living in the busy town of Oak Ridge, Tennessee, fifteen miles away, during the war years.

The house sat on a twenty-five foot bluff above Highway 70 which led to Knoxville. Across the road was a small grocery store, one gas pump and the home of our nearest neighbors, who just happened to have eleven children. They occasionally sold used cars, which the father and his older sons drove to Kingston from Detroit, and there was a large cage with a monkey living in it for a tourist attraction. What was not to like? Easy shopping, a tiny zoo and a mixture of instant friends of all ages.

The first thing my parents did was to begin redesigning the house. Inside the home, there was much moving of walls and creating arched doorways, of which they were fond, having lived many years in California. Dad rewired everything, hung sheetrock, replaced windows, added a studio for mom and introduced indoor plumbing including a proper bath, with the help of his dad who drove from Florida to assist.

It was the indoor plumbing that precipitated Mother falling into an old cistern that was hidden behind the house. My parents wanted to find a better source of water and were looking for a divining rod, a special tree branch, that was supposed to sense a good supply of water. Mother climbed up on a low structure and disappeared. She had fallen about fifteen to twenty feet into an abandoned cistern. Despite the trauma and drama of that moment, my parents did eventually find an excellent source of water, so good and cold that it could almost frost a glass in the summertime.

They made many improvements over the years. Most specifically was the stonework they both designed and created, using Tennessee Crab Orchard stone, to develop vertical flower beds, walkways and patios around the house.

My parents created a gentle life on those seven and a half acres. Mom painted in her studio, on the walls of our home, and planted gardens. Dad experimented with raising small livestock, stone masonry and gardening. All of us kids attended school and roamed the hills with our friends.

Mother took up pipe smoking. She favored the curved ones with carvings around the bowls. She called each one "Sebastian" and had a special blend of tobacco made for her in Knoxville. I think that was an effort to stop smoking cigarettes, but she decided she liked the attention. When my parents really wanted to cause a riot while traveling, they would take on a hillbilly vernacular LONG before the Beverly Hillbillies thought to use it! Mom would light up her pipe, and they would sprinkle you'enses and we'enses, pappy and mammys throughout their conversations while traveling through Pennsylvania and New York. I thought one gas station attendant was going to wipe the windshield away, he was so transfixed by what he was watching and hearing inside the car. And so began our Tennessee transformation, both in physical circumstances and language adjustments.

Mother, having grown up in California, was mesmerized by any snowfall. She often would wake us up during the night, when it had fallen heavily on her world, to see the miracle. We had visited friends up the road one evening with her, after a snowfall, and because all traffic had stopped due to the depth of the snow, we were walking down the middle of Highway 70. Mom started singing the song Mule Train and of course, we three children joined her. Loudly. Because the snow was deep and was covering the trees, land and buildings, it offered an odd acoustics umbrella of sound that echoed in the quietness of the twilight. We watched as porch lights came on and doors opened. People watched as our traveling road show mushed down the road. "Oh," I heard someone say. "It's just Peggy and her kids."

That was also the landscape in which we learned or rejected the mores and attitudes of those around us. We occasionally saw from our school buses the burned shapes of crosses on the lawns of our friends and neighbors. The children on the bus would become quiet and whisper.

We asked, "What is that? Why is that there?"

Most often they would tell us that someone in that home had been seen associating with a black person and were being 'warned'. We were concerned, because there were Negros in this small town, we lived in who had learned to love our mother. They would wait on the corners in town for her to make her way to them, knowing that she was always going to stop and chat. I would be impatient, wanting to get on with what we had come to do, but to her, that was the more important event. I can still see the look on their faces. They were friends to her and happy to see her, understanding that being accepted was a struggle for her, too. She carried herself in such an aspect of unawareness of her physical handicaps that others soon couldn't see them, either. So that was how she treated everyone.

There also was an area where we became teenagers and learned about dating, local boyfriends, smoking and drinking … or not. A favorite hang-out in town was called The Hut, which was mostly famous for its chili. The best-known food drive-in was Belly Acres. Until Kingston was blessed with an outdoor drive-in theater, there was only a small single-roomed theater (I think it was called The Fox), which in the winter was heated by a small pot-bellied coal stove up front, near the screen, and cooled in the summer by opening a door. Fortunately, the outdoor theater was installed by the time we had entered high school. Remember the huge circular poodle skirts, paired with sweaters featuring a false collar? And the boys in their dark jeans and white tee-shirts with their cigarette packs rolled up into the sleeve? That was us. The original

"Grease" prototypes. The boys would ride their bicycles the three and a half miles to our home, often leaving notes or little gifts in the Route 2 mailbox at the bottom of our hill, for my sister and me.

The Day Mother Disappeared

Mother is gone. We were all standing right there near her, but she is gone, missing, not in sight. My dad began shouting her name and twisting around, turning, trying to find her. A male friend standing near us looked puzzled and confused. All of us children were frozen in place.

It all began after my parents bought a home outside a small town. It was a typical small house on seven acres, near a mildly important road. The house had running water from a spigot outside, water in the kitchen, a bath, and electricity. That was the extent of its utility luxuries. Much to my dad's delight, the property also included a pig pen, chicken coop, and a smoke-house. There were many possibilities for experimenting.

For some reason, my dad wanted to have a new well drilled. They invited Mr. Evans, a man who knew about finding water underground, to help them determine where to drill. Mr. Evans used 'a divining rod' to do that. It was a small, forked limb, shaped like a long slender slingshot that was supposed to tug down towards the ground when it sensed water. Peach tree limbs were supposedly the best.

We were all walking around the house looking at trees for such a use when Mom noticed a peach tree. There was a low structure beside it, so she climbed up on it. Her paralyzed arm was tucked up near her body and she started pointing straight up at a limb she thought was perfect. That's when the top of the cistern she was standing on gave way, and she fell twenty-five feet down into it. We found her by her screams. "Get me out of here! Get me out of here! There are dead things down here!"

The two-and-a-half feet of water in the cistern had broken her fall. My dad used his bare hands to tear a bigger opening in the cement and steel rods that were capping the old well.

"Peggy! Peggy!" he kept screaming. "I'm OK! Just get me out of here!"

By that time, all of us children were hysterical, crying and holding on to each other.

My dad is looked at Mr. Evans and said, "We need a rope."

Now my mother had special problems: She was handi-capped and, only able to use one side of her body.

Mr. Evans remembered seeing a swing near the house. They ran to cut it down and fashioned a seat for her to sit on. They were able to pull her out of the cistern that way. She kept reas-suring everyone she was not harmed, only that the water was cold, dirty and had 'things' floating in it. By that time, all of us children were really sobbing, while Dad and Mr. Evans were shaking like leaves.

After being hosed down outside to get rid of the initial debris, Mother poured the men glasses of 'courage rewards' and left us to bathe away the rest of what lurked in the bottom of wells. I remember the conversations. Mostly about, "What if." What if both arms had been extended? They would have been broken. What if the water had been deeper or nonexistent? Snakes? We will never forget her experience. When my dad returned to the spot later to recap it, the material he had torn away with his bare hands, he now had to use a crowbar and hammer to dislodge the concrete and metal bars.

Some days are just more fun than others.

A Mixed Bag

Outside of a dog, a book is
man's best friend. Inside of
a dog it's too dark to read.
Groucho Marx

ANDY

It was Christmas Day. I was making a phone call and trying to speak through a stopped-up nose, while avoiding looking at my red eyes and unhappy face. Our pet of seven years had passed away suddenly. That may sound odd, but the pet was a two-and-a-half-pound dwarf bunny we had named Andy … a remarkably intelligent, intuitive creature that had totally stolen our hearts.

He was an 'impulse buy' at a local pet store. They had set him up with a cage and toys to show the simplicity of owning such a pet. He was tan with tiny charcoal stripes around his body. I later learned the description identified him as Hungalarian in the rabbit world, plus his sharp, short ears and the requisite white fluffy tail.

The 'catch' was that he came over to sniff and lick our fingers. It was meant to be. They told us it was a female, so we named him Annie. Later, we took him to the vet for a check-up. The vet disclosed our error. My husband, while walking through the waiting room with the cage, proudly announced,

"When we came in my rabbit was an Annie. We are going home with an Andy. My rabbit has had a sex change!" Someone said, "Rabbits are like that."

We took him home with a list for caring and feeding, a water bottle, food and a few instructions, which later were laughably inadequate. He was fearless and bossy from the first. I became his "woman" when he fell in love with a pair of blue fluffy slippers I had. My husband was a tolerated enemy whom he nipped in the face as often as he could. We finally had to have him neutered to reduce the number of scars my husband was collecting.

Andy was incredibly teachable. I bought cat balls that had slits in them and rolled them to him. He would pick up the balls with his teeth and with both front paws throw them back to me! I had lined up some boxes in an area to contain him one time. I saw him pacing the perimeter of those boxes, looking right, left and up.

Backing up a few steps, with a mighty leap, he gracefully sailed over all of them. I would not have believed it if I had not seen it. Those boxes were eighteen inches high and wide. He was very time oriented. He would put himself to bed at exactly 8:00 p.m. every night, including making the yearly time changes. What moments of fun he provided just being himself, tearing around the perimeters of a room with occasional, loud, thudding bangs from those big feet punctuating his progress. When he was entirely pixilated, he would leap high into the air to twist and cavort his little body into amazing contortions to show his happiness of the moment. Did you know that bunnies can purr? They do it by grinding their teeth. And he dearly loved dandelion greens, especially when I hid a little extra surprise food treat for him to find in them. He would climb the stairs to join me in my studio for a while during the day, and he always came out to greet any guests.

He had several eye problems so we took him to an animal oculist. One of those times we were waiting for the doctor, I was cradling Andy on the examining table when he walked in. He stood and watched us for a moment and then said, "He knows that he is loved."

Those few words said it all.

SENG

"We gave our dog away. How could we have done that? What kind of people were we?!'

I'll tell you what we were. We were five intimidated, clueless, un-dog-trained, miserable, seemingly hapless humans.

It seemed like an answer to an empty spot in our family to get a puppy for our three-year-old son. The two older boys were in school and he only had the companionship of Jemima, a neighbor child who lived on the other side of the hedges. We loved the excited day, driving in the English countryside to look at the pups. Beautiful Lhasa Apsos, four little tan fur balls bouncing around inside a pen. We were overwhelmed by the history being told to us by the owner-breeders. These were not ordinary pups. They were descended from royalty. Literally. They had been inside China for thousands of years (we were told) and only in recent times were allowing some outside the country. They were raised to be companions, roamed palaces and sat inside the long sleeves of clothing to keep the owners warm. Lion Dogs. Dignified, royal, respected. Those words would come back to haunt us.

The first mistake was in not studying raising, training and living with a dog. We thought past experiences would be enough. Enthusiasm carried us along for a while until the reality of living and getting on with our lives took over. What a beautiful thing he was—perfectly majestic, lovely furry body, lively, fun and almost bark-less. But he had a dark side. And we had stupid sides. His outranked ours. We absolutely could not house-break him. He piddled on everything in sight. Walls, floors, beds, clothing, even people's legs were targets. We walked that little dog so much that he was trembling to strain one more little squirt out to dominate the world with his scent. And then would come home to wet in inappropriate spots once more. We yelled "on the paper!" at him so often that it became a cliché. We would almost have fist fights before entering the house because it was an unwritten rule that whoever saw the mess first, had to clean it up.

We had a couple who often babysat the boys when we made trips. They in their younger years raised, trained and housebroke each pup before sending them home with the new owners. They worked the entire week with Seng and pronounced him a Dirty Dog when we returned. Apparently, that's where the term Dirty Dog came from—a pet who was impossible housebreak.

We begged people for help and information. Britishers are known for their well-trained and obedient dogs. The last straw was when Seng climbed up onto one of the beds and did a big pile of business there.

Coward that I was, I put an ad in the local newspaper: "Child allergic to dog. Free to a good home." Never mind that Lhasa Apsos are hyper-allergenic not having fur but hair. For some reason, he had no further problems from that moment. We wondered if he had read the ad in the papers on the kitchen floor: "Let's see. Dog food is a good price this week—I can continue to eat. There is a Fair downtown on the weekend. Wait! What's this!!! A dog-giveaway?!!!"

A kind, portly German lady came to see him. She was a 'walker,' she said, and loved to walk the hills and needed a companion. Perfect, I thought he would have endless opportunities to do what he needed. She took him, and I called occasionally to see how they were doing. "Wonderful," she said in a strong German accent, "we have many walks. And I take him to the butchers where I buy him ox-cheeks!" That little dog must have thought he had moved into heaven. He finally had the circumstances to show that he COULD be dignified, royal and respectable.

Ox-cheeks. Who would have thought of that?

My Dog Skip

My husband and I went to see the movie, *My Dog Skip*, and we were caught off-guard by the extremely touching story that was told. I could hear people sniffling all around us and was aware that I was having a very hard time trying not to cry as the movie neared the end. I could hear my husband's breath catching in his throat as the sad story unfolded, and he tried to hold back his tears.

I think everyone was doing well, even though we all seemed to want to sit in our seats a moment after the lights came on. Then, somewhere down in the middle of the theatre, in the dim light, a young voice started sobbing as if his little heart was breaking. That did it. It seemed that everyone in the room began to cry, including us. There was just something about that young child's wailing, somewhere in the middle of the crowd, that gave us all permission to let it out. There was no way we could hold it in any longer.

We all looked at each other while leaving, most with shy

smiles and tears still wet on our faces. Many parents were still trying to comfort their children. "There was just no holding that in!" one older gentleman said, while still wiping his eyes and smiling.

THE WARRIOR PRINCESS

The room is cool, quiet and still a little dark.

I look down at my Shih Tzu, lying stretched out in her bed on the floor beside me. We all have natural alarm clocks, even animals. Mine is 6:45 A.M. every day of the world, if I don't tamper with it. She knows she has to wait while I fumble for my robe and slippers and brush my teeth before she can go outside to take care of her morning needs. So, she stays quietly in her bed occasionally watching to make sure I am on schedule, pushing one little eyebrow up, as she opens that eye to check my progress.

Because I recently had knee surgery, I'm slower than usual so now I have to gather up all I will need during the day and put these items on my rollator, to travel with them around the house. That includes a bottle of pills, my phone, a list of daily exercises, a cane and Zena's bed piled on top, which I will return to her spot by my chair, in the family room.

My son is staying with us during my forced incarceration,

and he is taking care of all of Zena's outside needs. This morning we are slower than usual because I also need help putting on my compression stocking, before he takes her out. There is no way I can put that thing on by myself. It's a little like trying to stuff your leg into a boa constrictor while also trying to leave a little room for your toes. Unfortunately, it's been done inside-out and has to be re-done. My son turns the stocking to the right side and does it again, stopping to create a little entertainment with 'this little piggy went to market' scenario ending with 'the last little piggy stopping somewhere for Chicken and Waffles.' Zena crawls back into her bed and doggie-glares at what she now seems to be considering as Looney-Tunes going on.

I wheel my walker to the kitchen and begin my 'Job One' of preparing Zena's breakfast. My son has the back door open and is describing the wonders of the great outdoors for Zena's consideration. "The gardener has been here, Madame, and everything is pristine and weed-free for your inspection and pleasure in the main courtyard," he tells her. She gives him the Shih-Tzu-Eye and stares from the nose-down position from her bed. It is not going to be a speedy day.

"Ah so," he says, "we will wait."

Eventually, nature intervenes, and she moves towards the door. Zena is an eleven-year-old dog, and it usually doesn't take long for natural urges to keep her on track. She knows she is going to get a carrot slice when she does well, and another carrot slice when she eats most of her meal. It is a confession I haven't told many. I pay my dog to eat. It seems to work for us. When she was a puppy, she had many food allergies, and it was a trial for the vet to find food to which she wasn't sensitive.

Most brands made her look like she was trying to rip her skin off while scratching.

She is a dear, intrusive little presence, able to keep us tuned into her needs and enchant us the rest of the time with her endless perceptions and opinions of us and our activities. Most obvious is her ability to mold us into her constant servants and entertainers. I have often described myself as her social director. She is very fussy about when she is petted and by whom. We have a phrase that describes those moments: *Don't Touch! I am being regal today, and you have not qualified to pet 'The Puppy' yet.*

She has always liked other dogs and goes into various yards to bump noses with neighborhood cats. I have never seen her harass any of the squirrels outside. They seem to look up from their acorn-digging and meals to stare, without interrupting their munching. "Oh, it's only Zena." I have observed over the years that she favors men. What would a fellow not like in all that cuteness? She runs to them so they can run their hands through her fur and scratch her ears. When she was a puppy, men actually stopped their cars in the middle of the road and left the engines running, with the doors standing open, to run over and ask, "May I pet your little puppy?" I don't know what to call that, but she had it, even back then.

She is on file as Zena Warrior Princess with the American Kennel Club. Every time we introduced her to people as "Zena", they would invariably add Warrior Princess, with a happy smile. It seemed to make sense to include those two names. Her mother is named Ya Ya Divine. I kind of like that one, too.

She recently developed pancreatitis and spent twelve days in the Animal Emergency Hospital. It was terrifying to see her little legs shaved so ports could be put into them to supply the medications and nutrients she would need. I was able to take her home, the vet thought, after the first two days of treatment, but I hurried her back to them the next day. She was crashing again. I went to her, two times each day to hand-feed her or to hold her in my lap, or to simply be in the room, when she didn't want to be handled or eat. Her usually pristine fur was often matted and messy, even though the technicians tried to keep her tidy. I took wet and dry cloths each time to try to help them keep her clean.

How sad it was to sit with her and think of all the tiny moments over the years, that meant so much, and try to steady myself should she get worse. My friends were wonderful and stayed in touch each day, calling to ask how she was doing.

Finally ... finally, she turned the corner and began to get well. It was a slow process, but she began reacting to us and showing up at her food bowl again. I can't look at her in the same way, this faithful little companion. I now have new parameters to consider regarding her place in my life. She is even more precious, and I am more aware of the truly short time we have with these little creatures who move along beside us each day.

You Never Know

Life is like riding a bicycle.
To keep your balance,
you have to keep moving.
Albert Einstein

How To Throw
A Party ... Or Not

When we moved to England, we were "sponsored" by a family whose responsibility it was to indoctrinate us into the where-ares, how to get-tos and basically how to begin to understand being in another country. They were a kind, generous, sympathetic couple with a small boy, who helped us with all that we needed to find.

There were many needs that were immediate: Find a rental for a family of five, decide which school our young teens would attend and buy uniforms for said school. Shopping was so different with shopping companies referred to by nicknames and items were not where we normally would buy them, such as post offices that sold dog licenses. There was so much to discover, and this dear couple did their best to help us blend in and learn.

They took us to outings, meetings and introduced us to other Americans and British friends. They chauffeured us to many places until we found a small British Minor car to drive until our American car arrived from the States. They baby-sat my eighteen-month-old when I had activities to be done without him. They became close friends and when it was time for them to rotate back to their home in the states, I wanted to give them the best party I could put together. A party that they would never forget and always remember.

I had another close friend who was up for helping me plan this farewell. Now I have to explain something. As can happen in close communities, there are often competing factions and not always in a good way. One such faction was military and the other was civilian. There were often fistfights and other physical displays of aggression especially after the consumption of a few British beers. So, to discourage any of this behavior, we decided to make it a formal party. Men would wear suits and women, would wear gowns.

My friend and I spent many hours planning the buffet menu, drinks and desserts. We talked another friend into hosting the event. She had a spectacular home in the hills and the evening twinkling lights of the beautiful town below were visible from the house and gardens. We pictured an elegant evening in that magnificent setting.

The big day arrived. The women spent time at the hairdressers. They laid their evening wear out on their beds, putting all their jewelry and accessories together they had probably been choosing for weeks. The men did what they do to look their best in suits and ties. They began arriving slowly, up the hill, parking the cars, and staying outside for a moment to look at the incredible views down the hill. Inside the home, we had arranged the bars, appetizers, and beautifully done platters and dishes of local extravagant food choices. In our eyes, it was magnificent. Along with our host's home and furnishings, it indeed looked well done. We felt we had buffered the evening with good intentions and good looks.

The women were at their best, knowing they were lovely to look at, walking around in their long gowns talking quietly with tinkling laughs. The men had done whatever that magic is that makes them look almost as exciting as their wives. Our guests of honor were over-whelmed and appreciated the efforts we had made for their final social send-off.

But then, some late comers arrived, with their imbibing already in progress, and were obviously a little on the testy side. Some of the men met them with quiet words and remind-ed them that this was to be a compatible evening even though some shared bad tempers over past disagreements. It looked as though it was going to work. They blended in and most of us began dancing to the music and enjoying the tables and side-boards of temptations.

But, alas, it began as a low rumble. Bad comments followed by other retorts, some shoving, and then it happened so fast no one could tell where it began. It seemed to erupt all over the room. Men shouting, yelling, throwing blows, punching, and knocking each other around. The women stood shocked, just watching. Thank goodness for the very tall window openings in the room. They provided an exit for the fighting to tum-ble into the outside garden. We women stood at the windows, holding onto each other's arms, not believing what we were seeing. Half of the men were trying to break it up and calm them down all while getting hit in the process. Others were still throwing punches, banging heads, rolling around on the ground.

I'm not sure how or why all the commotion finally stopped. People were bleeding, clothing torn, and some of the men were covered in dirt from rolling in the flower beds. The women stood quietly, not able to believe what had happened. Thankfully, the fighting had moved outside, saving the beautiful home from destruction. I just have a faint memory of people slowly straightening up, mumbling apologies, and men trying to straighten their clothing and cars beginning to leave.

Apparently, the Head Director of the American group in London heard about what happened and called the offenders into his office the next morning. I can only imagine what transpired, but I know that for most of the next day our doorbell was constantly ringing. Men with black eyes, bandages and shamed faces showed up with apologies, commanded to do so by the Director.

I don't remember any more fistfights going on after that. At least, not out in the open. We had the distinction of having our well-intentioned party-fiasco transmitted around the world via the Internet. It was legend. After we returned home, when people heard our names, it was always "Oh … aren't you the ones who gave … The Party?"

But we did give our friends an evening that they would always remember.

HALLOWEEN

I remember in the '60s when having a Key to The Bunny Club making one a member, was an exotic event for young marrieds. My husband and I would dress for the evening and go with friends to The Bunny Club in Baltimore, Maryland. There we would have dinner, while being entertained by an exceptionally good band, and the beautiful Bunnies would serve our meals. The constraints of being a Mommy and Daddy would fall away for a while.

One night after having dinner there and enjoying what was a "new" combination of foods at that time, Surf and Turf which was a lobster and a steak (I did say that this was the '60s), we decided to extend our evening by looking around town to see what else there was to do. Someone remembered reading that Blaze Starr was playing a limited engagement at one of the night clubs. Well, the six of us headed over there to see what was going on.

Blaze was an entertainer of extremely specific attributes, most to do with her physical appearance. I remember being surprised that she was a very petite woman. Her style of enter-taining was immortalized in the movie "*Gypsy*", about a dancer called Gypsy Rose Lee.

As usual, it was dark and smoky in the night club, but we found seats close to the stage and settled in to see what she was all about. I must have led a more sheltered life than I had realized, because I was entranced by her appearance more than anything. At that time, I think she was nearing the end of her career and was probably not as excited about her routine, which while interesting, was perhaps beginning to show she needed retirement. I left, thinking about all that I had seen.

The following week was Halloween. The night of Trick or Treat was very busy. While my husband was answering the door and handing out treats, I sneaked upstairs, having decid-ed to dress myself in a costume as well. I wanted to do a comic routine of Blaze Starr: I teased my hair up as high and far out as it would go, drew black lines around my eyes with huge eyelashes, rouged my cheeks and applied the reddest lipstick I had, in an exaggerated outline. Then I stuffed the front of my shirt until it could hold no more stuffing. Feeling as if I had done a good rendition, I headed back downstairs to surprise my husband.

I didn't see the couple he was greeting at the door as I walked up behind him, but there stood our new neighbors with their two small sons. I realized my predicament and stayed behind him while he said hello. Unfortunately, he realized that I was there and at some point, turned and said, "And this is my wife ..."

I will never forget the look on their faces as I was revealed in all my 'Blaze Starr' glory.

Exit Stage left.

HALLOWEEN BUNNIES

While in England for three years, I remember that I had more available time to do as I pleased. It was different to fill my days with unusual activities and be able to choose what I was going to do each day, because I did not work when living there. Perhaps, I had a little too much free time.

I had three sons, who were four, twelve and fourteen at that time. The American holiday of Halloween was coming up and they needed costumes for individual parties, as I did. After having gone as a ghost the year before, I decided to try a different approach. The ghost idea had been easy with two eye holes cut appropriately in a white sheet with a sheer layer of material over it that wafted around when moving.

That year I thought I would make a fluffy pink bunny out-fit. It was on the order of a Playboy Bunny, with a big fluffy tail and a head piece with huge pink ears. I found the longest, most sappy-looking eyelashes to wear. That, plus high heels, lacy hose, and I was good-to-go.

The twelve-year-old decided that he would like to wear the

costume also. He was about my size so with dark leggings, his grimy tennis shoes, and dark ghoulish make-up, he was a perfect teenage-zombie pink bunny.

My four-year-old also wanted to wear a bunny outfit. I padded it out, so he was a plump little bunny complete with whiskers and a cherub face. Adorable. I have to brag a little … all three outfits won First Prize at their parties.

The first Halloween, I remember taking only the oldest boy out trick or treating years before in Maryland. His brother had a cold and was too ill to go. I worked at the time and had gotten home late. Buying costumes was not an option in the '60s. I told my anxious son that we had to find something around the house for him to wear. So help me, the fastest thing I could come up with was a Carmen Miranda-look. I had a bowl of plastic fruit on the table which gave me the idea. Bandana on the head, fruit pinned to that, a large shirt over his coat (it was cold outside) and a long skirt, flashy make-up and we stepped outside. The biggest blessing he had going for him was that we were new in the neighborhood and no one recognized him. The lure of all that chocolate and candy given away made him desperate enough to wear anything. Thank goodness his father wasn't home yet to ask if I had lost my mind.

Another year, I made huge spiders out of wrapping paper tubes and almost asphyxiated myself painting them black in the garage. I hung three of them on the small entry porch, and the two oldest boys sat on the top of the porch and manipulated them as small children dressed as creatures came to the door. It was too realistic … most of them screamed and ran.

I do remember one little Superman retreating with his cape flying behind him.

I chased after them all and filled their bags generously with Halloween sweets and apologies.

EARTHQUAKE

It was dusky outside. That time of day when the sun still lights objects, but shadows are beginning to deepen and lengthen. It was about 5:30 P.M. in Anchorage, Alaska, Good Friday Eve. I was standing outside the back entrance to the private x-ray department where I worked, waiting for my husband and two children to pick me up.

We had lived in Anchorage almost three years and had often experienced rumblings of the earth, but this was different. It started with a low moan and a gentle waving of the ground. The moan became louder and the waves more pronounced, as if they would be, moving across an ocean. The doctor I worked for ran outside just as the ground was beginning to pitch wildly, making the cars nearby rock up and down and back and forth as if they were floating on water. We kept falling down and helping each other back up. The noise was so loud we couldn't hear each other speak. Pieces began to fall off the building.

Other sounds were the telephone wires zinging as the poles pitched back and forth, like ship spars in a wild ocean. There were explosions as transformers blew up. In the distance we could see dark clouds of dust as houses imploded and fell.

I wondered where my husband was and what was happening to him along with our two and four-year-old children.

He had just entered the one-story building where I worked and was in a hallway, carrying one child, and he held the other by his hand. As the earthquake intensified the walls touched them on both sides. He had turned and tried to run outside. A wall was leaning on him at one point, but he exited finally with both children screaming. One had lost a boot and was hysterical about it.

The quake lasted 4.5 minutes and was a 9.2 on the Richter Scale, the second most powerful one to ever happen. We learned later that lakes in Texas sloshed around in their beds and that the entire earth had rung like a bell.

We were able to drive the few miles to our home, avoiding holes and cracks in the roads. The electricity was out, but our home was standing. Eventually the radio said the water in our area was safe. The inside of the house looked as if it had been violently shaken with everything out of the closets and drawers, furniture askew, and the washer and dryer had moved across the room. Every piece of china, glass and crystal was broken.

People behave differently when there is a disaster. I saw that we all wanted to be with someone. I had two other families staying with me for three days, one of them had indeed lost their home. For some reason, we all wanted to be in the same room together. We slept in chairs, sofas, sleeping bags and blankets made beds in the corners of the rooms for the five children. The aftershocks were nerve-wracking. We learned later many homes along the Cook Inlet had been swallowed up or fell into the bay. One of the worst events was the tsunamis that struck Seward, Alaska, about twenty-five miles east of us. It was located around a small bay and when the tsunamis entered the area, it swirled in a flushing motion carrying everything on the rim to the bottom of the bay. That included trains and tracks, homes and businesses.

Because Sunday was Easter, the other mothers and I hid the Easter Eggs, baskets and goodies we had all around the house for the children to find that morning. Even in the midst of disaster, we wanted to do something that felt normal.

Hurricane Bejabbers

You stand and look at all your stuff in disarray: Paintings in black garbage bags, sealed with duct tape and leaning on walls; important papers to travel with you, out of their usual filing places, stuffed into a water-proof clear box; the baby grand standing beneath a taped-together cover of garbage bags; and all your written stories are safely tucked into another clear plastic box. Some items are hidden ... hope I can remember where. You've moved fragile pieces to what are hopefully safer places to weather a storm. Suddenly your home is a-bloom with all the flowering pots from outside sitting around your entrance room and in the garage, so they won't become flying projectiles.

I've done this so many times over the years. After living through Hurricane Andrew, a Category Five, in southwest Florida, we carefully asked before moving to North Carolina, "When was the last hurricane in here?" Twenty-three years was the answer. Yes! We can move here. Then three hurricanes promptly monster-mashed their way across Wilmington and parts west.

There are piles of traveling gear in the hallway, waiting for their places in the car: All of the dog's needs and her travel cage; computers and technical supports; a bag of my entertainments (knitting, books, magazines) and a wicker basket filled with snacks, maps, TV guide, drinks, charging cables for the phones, address books and all the things I have learned are necessary for running away.

I take one last look around the house, as I have done so many times before, and wonder what it is going to be like when I return. Parts blown away? Roof half off? Windows blown in? I then put the garage door down and drive away from my home, hoping for mercy.

Later, I'm glued to the television and my phone for the next eight days, the longest I have ever stayed away. This storm, Florence, was different. It spent several days over very warm water gathering strength and looked fierce. It shrank from a Category Five to a Two. It still makes me uneasy. Newscasters are warning people to beware, it was forecasted to be an historical rainmaker. And it is. Reports of flooding were astonishing and heart-rending. Many incredible stories were relayed over and over on television with videos of families clinging to trees and their rooftops. Neighbors were beginning to send pictures of the destruction when they could safely get out of their homes. Unfortunately, mine was one of the stricken.

As we drove back, there was a smattering of evidence, while still five hours away, of the ravages of Florence, and it steadily increased as we got closer. We were being diverted and managed by the State Highway Patrol to where we could travel. Most roads east were underwater, but we steadily made our way north to Highway 17, where we were able to drive east again to Wilmington.

Driving past Topsail and Hampstead, we began to get an idea of what might be ahead. And it was. When we turned into our community, the roads had been cleared for only one-lane travel on most streets. There were huge piles and drifts of cut-up logs, branches, leaves and treetops along the roads, in yards and around homes. Some of the debris piles were so tall, I could not see the houses. We were softly saying "Look at that ... and that ... and THAT." The destruction had clearly included almost everyone, in one way or another. As we turned onto our cul-de-sac, I could not see my house at all, because the pile of vegetation along the curb was twice as tall as I. A tree had fallen onto the left side of my home. I knew that it had, because neighbors had sent me photos of it, lifted out of the ground and leaning there. There was another large oak tree on the right side that had come up by its roots also, and fallen on the community fence, crushing it and opening large blocks of space. I was very lucky both trees had already been cut into logs and piled up. We had just enough room to park the car in the driveway.

I knew my kind neighbors had been able to get inside my home and into the attic. One of them sawed off limbs sticking through the roof and put spray foam into the openings. Another neighbor and his wife had cleared out my master bedroom clothes' closet because water had been running down the bathroom ceiling onto the floor. That was above and beyond the call of gentle neighborliness and I knew I couldn't thank them enough. There had been a lot of stuff in that closet. One of the neighbors had put a sheet of plastic covering over one of my bookshelves in the office, in case the water should travel in that direction. Such kindnesses would be impossible to repay.

The next morning there was someone knocking on my door to say, "You have one of the biggest piles of debris, and we are going to clear yours out first." Another blessing. I could then see my neighbor's house. My two sons patched the five holes they found on the roof as well as, the gash in the siding with products they bought before returning.

So, I, along with hundreds and thousands of others, spent time on our phones trying to find people to repair our homes and redo the landscaping, which included cutting down more damaged trees. It was wonderful to know that the stores and gas stations were restocking, and businesses and services were beginning to return to normal. I later saw the garbage truck pick up my trash bin. I knew we were almost there.

NEW YEAR'S EVE

You know, after the clock strikes 12:00, it's pretty much over. I remember one New Year's Eve party, glancing at my husband after midnight and being startled by the fact that he was holding one eye open with his fingers and apparently trying to sleep with the other one.

We were in the basement of someone's home in Anchorage, Alaska. The room was typical of a couple in our age group, made up to be a 'den', very comfy with overstuffed furniture, a small fireplace and a bar/kitchen. The 60s music was loud and conversations even more so. The fireplace, while being picturesque, was beginning to heat up the room. All of us had traveled through minus 32-degree temperatures to get there and were suitably dressed should any outdoor emergency arrive. Trays of food were passed around. Unfortunately, everyone smoked back then so the room was filled with acrid cigarette smoke. Guests began to get mellow due to Happy New Year's drinks and sweat began to be a problem. Most shed their heavy hand-knitted sweaters and a few took off their boots.

Just about the time we had all hit a new level of heat and alcohol endurance, there was a strange odor in the room. I wasn't sure what it was, but the room was suddenly wet-dog steamy, and not from the woolen sweaters. The hosts had put a big pot of black-eyed peas on the stove to cook. Think about it. That's not an odor that goes well with food, steam, alcohol and an already overstimulated tummy. All I longed for was a breath of fresh air, even air that was minus 32-degrees and would freeze the inside of your nose (which might have been an advantage). But there was no escaping. The hosts maintained that it was traditional to eat those peas on New Year's Eve to insure prosperity in the coming year. Unfortunately, they took an inordinate amount of time to finish cooking. How terrific it would have been if they had been cooked beforehand, or even if they had put some ham or sausage in for seasoning. Anything but that stark aroma. Sniffing ham or sausage would have been preferable to the peas. Sitting around, wishing to go home to my bed, long after midnight, when the evening is truly past its function and intention, was not a good thing. Especially with every nook and cranny filled with the aroma of fresh black-eyed peas still cooking. I was ready to give up any prosperity for the year just to be able to go home.

Another New Year's was spent on board a luxury cruise ship. It was beautifully decorated for the holiday seasons and loaded with every festivity by both the cruise company and the people who were on board. Every costume and idiom of the season had been brought on board and fleshed out by the ship's crews and cooks, including magnificent meals, entertainment and activities. Everyone was working hard to impress and entertain.

The biggest event of the cruise, of course, was New Year's Eve. The guests and crew dressed for the evening and the dining rooms were resplendent with extravagantly prepared meals and dishes. The guests twinkled with sparkles in their hair and clothing. There was soft pink lighting that made everyone look 30 years younger and we all fell under the spell. We gorged and indulged and then did it again. We were stuffed full of what I can wish to remember but can only come up with the impression that was made. Lovely, ornate, aromatic, creative, glorious foods. And we, the participants, were like geese being prepared to make pate. At least, that's what I felt like at the end of the evening.

In all fairness, we did know about the midnight Chocolate Extravaganza the cooks had probably spent months preparing. There were tables and tables of every chocolate fantasy we could possibly imagine, waterfalls, candies, cakes, statues, every chocolate-coated thing known to man. Faces, fairies, storybook characters, amazing artwork drizzled and fizzled and twirled everywhere.

I had a little Dachshund once, who, if she could find enough food, would eat until she exploded. I often thought when she would escape and rummage through garbage cans, and her skin was so tight when she returned, if I touched her, she would rip like a zipper. That's how I felt at that moment at the chocolate buffet. Don't touch! Gluttony is never a pretty sight.

And I felt that I was too old to be making such obviously bad food decisions ... but New Year's always gives one the hope of redemption.

Now and Then

All you need is love.
But a little chocolate now
and then doesn't hurt.
Charles M. Schulz

GIRLFRIENDS

I was reflecting one day on the number of girlfriends I have had over the years, and the strength of the friends they were, at the time. I see now that they seemed to have arrived as needed and either stayed for the long haul or were nearby for the duration.

The first one to come to memory would be my sister, but all I can envision is her little self lying in her crib, with dark hair and a diaper. The next time my memory sees her is a year later. My parents had moved out into the country to Lake Worth, Florida. I was standing next to her as a truck backed over her little body. I was aware of people running and screaming and my Dad wrapping her into a blanket. After that she was not allowed out of her crib and Mother moved it around the house, so she could be with us. I'm guessing that was to keep her from walking at the time, but eventually Mother had to tie the crib to doorknobs when she learned how to 'pump' the crib from room to room by herself. Next scene is both of us having whooping cough in that house during a hurricane and our mother moving between the beds caring for us. I see now that my sister could easily have been taken from me.

After those years, we moved many times with our parents. She has always been my 'Most Important Friend' my entire life, as we moved through our destinies: attending schools, marrying, raising families and finally becoming senior citizens together. God has been generous, allowing us to travel our roads together, sharing our traumas and glorious healing laughter.

I think it might have been about the time of the third grade that friendships made a turn and became something different. They began to have different values. Different reasons for being accepted … or not. That is when I became aware of the 'Cool Kids' phenomena. Apparently, I was not one of that genre. That was when I felt the sting of not being 'chosen' for games or groups. The girls I admired spread their lunch trays out so there was no room at the table to accept me sitting with them.

I decided the answer to that behavior was to form my own gang. Easy enough to do. Those new girlfriends, myself, plus a few boys, became close throughout our high school years. When I now watch episodes of *Friends*, I see us in them.

Here and there, a special person would come alongside and leave their touches in my life, even though they might be there for only a short time. I'm thinking of Peggy. Her father was a construction worker and her family traveled with a trailer to his work areas. Can you think of the things you learned from your friends? Peggy smoothed the rough edges off my personality, I think. She was a classic young lady and I tended to be stubborn and competitive. Her gentle strength is still memorable to me.

During high school, my closest group became three individuals. We drew a tiny triangle with a "3" inside it for our signature motif. We put it everywhere. That was probably done to align ourselves with the five most popular, powerful boys in school who designated themselves with a large triangle and the number "5." At least, we felt considerable, with our self-assigned association.

Those were the young women I learned loyalty to friends from, and how to think about the latest styles of hair, skirts and sweaters, dates and any puzzling personal problems we found ourselves involved in. Those two were also the most brilliant girls I knew. They made me look good!

When I went off to school, I found a multitude of friends with whom I examined and explored being on one's own. Those were the mixed bag of rooming houses and shared rooms, of shared clothing, shared trips, experimentation in drinking, exploring the edges of our own morals, deciding what was important and what to let drift away. We learned caution and who and when to trust. We fought battles over nothing and then provided shoulders for others to lean on when circumstances became frustrating or when things became too hard to do alone. Those were the years that provided us the information, mind-sets and attitudes we were going to use pursuing our careers or lifestyles. When we left, we would be facing new directions and challenges. It was where I saw the often free-fall of young women who had no, or thin boundaries, and the consequences of their behavior. They were often exquisite and painful lessons to watch and learn from.

Next in my life was San Antonio, Texas. Married ... Pregnant ... A military wife. I met two of the most influential women of my life in that town. Karen taught me how to care for a baby, how to bake, and how to live gracefully. She taught by example how to be a wife, a mother and how to remember to nourish the parts that were yourself. The other friend, Linda, came vested with vast information of how to do everything under the sun. She was a genius at teaching and discovering how to make or invent anything in the world. Whether it was weaving, knitting, sewing, cooking, sculpting, or canning – she was continually exploring or creating new things or discovering new ways to do them. She was a magical mentor for me, inviting me to share her adventures in creativity. I was fortunate in that those two women were also stationed with their husbands at the next base assignment we were sent to. It was in Alaska. Karen continued her explorations of baking and frosting tutorials, along with storytelling, with me. Linda and I knitted, needlepointed and sewed every new discovery we could find for those three years. The lessons I learned from both of those two generous friends have followed me to this day.

England. I've noticed that I often divide my life into continents or states. England was a fairy tale of a move. I met many new friends, American and British, with whom I've had amazing experiences. One Brit, Sylvia, is a dear friend even today, 50 years later. I had an email from her just a few days ago. We're both aging as gracefully as we can, and exchange information based on what her cat has been up to, how grand or great-grandchildren are doing, or what she has made lately for one of her four dollhouses. I treasure her letters, filled with her British vernacular and humor, and celebrate that we both have made it to these ages, still in touch.

Next came an era of 'married friends.' They were neighbors, good and bad. One was a shooting star of activities that
entertained and fascinated. Others were the quiet friends I
found at my places of employment. One remarkable friend,
Joan, came alongside me after a divorce, remarriage and an
experience in learning that I could know God personally. She
wrote me letters, gave me books, had long talks, and helped me
walk through the destruction and the truly ultimate resurrec-
tion of my life. A move to Delaware followed and offered more
remarkable women that were added to my life, mentoring or
supporting the changes that were happening rapidly. I joined
the classes of Bible Study Fellowship and there found profound
friendships I have had for years. One of those ladies still sends
me prayers each night. How faithful some women are.

Of course, I have wonderful women to know, where I am
now. I am grateful for the ones who have been placed in my
life as I have moved along. I could only wish that they would
be able to feel about me, as I have about them … and know
that I have added some interest, fun or truth to their lives also.

It's Over

What a strange thought.

One spends most of one's life knowing what the plan is for tomorrow. What is going to happen next week, next year and on out into most of the future.

It's strange to think that your life as you knew it, is over. Nothing is going to be the same. Nothing from this moment on. It will be a whole new day, time, even life. It was such a huge thought, that I had to write it down, look at it, and try to grasp the whole meaning of what I was realizing.

Even the room felt different. Nothing looked or felt the same. I looked around, trying to absorb the facts of the circumstances. This is my home; it is familiar. And yet, it's indeed not the same place it was when I left a few hours ago. It feels as though something has come in and made erasures and, hasn't yet been determined what they are to be. I just have a strong awareness that it has been done and some things are gone.

I am thinking that I was not consulted about these differences. They have shown up on their own. They are there, waiting to be defined and noticed.

I am sitting here, simply letting these ideas and understandings wash over me. I am not aware that they are going to be like a tsunami, first drawing out to sea, then coming in gently, growing larger, higher, deeper, coming in faster with more depth and power until I feel I am under the pressure and weight of unseen waves with the heaviness of water.

Even so, I feel calm. I understand what has happened. I just didn't expect to meet the reality of it in such a way as this. I knew this day would happen. I walked along with it, doing what I could to hold it off, to try to make it easier, to form my thoughts and understanding of eventualities, against the day that it arrived.

But I am now understanding that no one can do this ahead of time. No one can wear the knowledge of how they will perform or react to the inevitable event. Even when they see it happening before their eyes.

There is a peacefulness along with the heaviness. A gratefulness that finally the worst is over. What is it called? It's an odd notion of being suspended in space and time at this moment. There is something missing, along with a powerful notion of a space that is now empty. It feels that even the air around me has an expectation of some kind.

I must think about this. Absorb it. Consider what is happening, where to begin, because there is obviously a need for a new beginning of some kind. I need to sit for a while, because when I get up, everything is going to begin to move in a new direction. Nothing will be the same.

I am intensely aware of my breathing. I am sitting still, not wanting to have anyone else around, not wanting anything to be required of me at this moment. It feels quiet and needful to sit here by myself. I need the quiet to settle myself. In the stillness, I can feel my spiritual Father comforting me with the softness of His feelings. I feel His caring for me, His tenderness at this moment. This is the worst moment of my life and He is here, as He always is.

I can get through this. I can move in that new direction now.

I left Hospice, where my husband had just died, two hours ago. I can make the phone calls now.

MARIE

The first time I saw her, she was pulling one of her sons down a sidewalk, who was laying on a platform with wheels. I stood at my living room window and watched, trying to determine what was going on. I could see that the boy looked to be about the age of my oldest son, who was eight. That boy was wearing a cast on one side of his body which covered his leg from hips to his ankle. Their progress looked smooth and comfortable, as if they had done it before.

A short time before, I had just moved into the community, that was between Baltimore and Annapolis in Maryland. Because I worked, I hadn't met many of my neighbors. The woman I was watching was tall, dark-haired and moved with a graceful purpose, even while tugging along her son. The boy looked as if he was happy about wherever they were going and watched ahead with a look of anticipation. I'm not sure my eight-year son old would have done the same. He would have argued me out of doing such an activity in public. So. I would have probably thought to take him somewhere in our car. Hmmm. I was really puzzled and intrigued at what I was seeing. So many questions. Why was she transporting him like that? Why was he in a cast? Where did they live? It was a school-day, so I wondered how long he had been in the cast that was obviously keeping him at home.

I'm not exactly sure how I finally met this boy and his mother. I did find out that she had another boy who was the age of my younger son, and they and her husband lived on the opposite side of the street about three houses down. I surely did not guess or understand this woman and I were destined to become friends who would be a part of each other's lives for many years. Our husbands would also ride together to work because they both were employed at Ft. Meade, Maryland.

The very first memory I have is offering to take her and her boys shopping, along with my two sons. There we were, the four boys in the back seat and Marie and I in the front. Her oldest son had recently his cast removed after having surgery on his hip for the second time due to a congenital deformity in his hip. As I was backing out of the driveway, his voice pipped up from the backseat, "Miss Diane." "Yes, Bobby?" I asked. "This is the first time my mother has left the house in a car without my dad," he continued. There was dead silence in the car. I looked at my friend and she was staring straight ahead. She then turned and nailed her son to the backseat with a look. That was the end of the discussion.

She told me later she had a morbid fear of being around people, alone, for years. She had received counseling and experimentation to overcome it, but so far nothing helped. The furthest thing she had gotten to do alone was to sit outside on her front step at night when no one was around. For some reason she trusted me and allowed me to share that world with her.

Her disability was a very strange phenomenon to me because she was one of the most well-adjusted, outgoing and engaging people I had ever met. Her background was that of a typical expressive Italian, and she would give anyone the pro-verbial 'shirt off her back' if she thought you needed it.

Her greatest talent was to create scenarios for us to enact and get involved in. For instance, we were living in the late '60s and it was the era of mini dresses and hair styles as high as you could get them. She found an in-home hairdresser (anoth-er expression of her inability to go out in public places) and took me with her. We both came home with the most stunning hairdos, piled high with curls. She bribed, cajoled or arm-wres-tled our husbands into taking us out that night. We were just too good to waste! We put on our shortest minis and went dancing. The DJ there even singled us out for special recog-nition. We truly felt lovely and unconquerable. Marie had the ability to make everyone feel beautiful and assured them they were having the best time of their lives. I told her often that if she could just believe in her own personality, she could take over the world.

I often wondered what demons caused her to behave in such a different way, to see herself differently from the way others saw her. Over the years I found reasons I thought might be causing her problems, but she chose to just live within her limits while making the extraordinary best of them. It was very hard for her to visit in someone else's home, so she would make hers as entertaining and fun as she possibly could. And she was very good at it. Her Christmas was an extravaganza. I could hardly wait to see what she had done. Her personal style of dressing was perfect for her. She was six feet tall, and she wore everything as if she was a model. She adored her two sons, and I could see why her son had handled his restrictions with such aplomb, having been given the confidence from his mother to overcome and ignore what he could not change at the time. Why she would not do that for herself, I could never understand.

We shopped, visited, played, laughed and got into minor troubles together, while always having great fun. Once I decided that I wanted to have a home perm. She offered to give me one, having done it many times for herself. What neither of us knew was that I had used a product called Sun-In to lighten my hair. The chemicals in the perm began reacting to the chemicals in the Sun-In. She had my hair up in the curlers and we were chatting over coffees while waiting for the reaction time to pass. In the meantime, my hair in the curlers began to stretch longer and longer, finally dropping off my head entirely. I can still see the look on her face as my hair kept dropping off my head. I called a hair dressing shop I had been to for haircuts and told them I was coming in with an emergency! They put three different neutralizers on before the perm action stopped. Most of the hair on one side was gone and the other was about one inch in length. They cut my hair as best they could. You know what … I liked it so much that I wore it way for years. In the meantime, until all the damage was finally cut away, the affected hair would become like stretchy, cooked spaghetti when I washed it.

Because of our husband's jobs, we were offered three-year tours to live in other countries. We decided to move to England and Marie and her family went to Australia. A very strange event happened. We did not stay in touch with each other during those three years, so we didn't know anything that was going on in each other's lives

One evening while my husband and I were driving into London to see the stage production of 'Hair', I began having a very real vision of someone struggling. I could see only their head. It was a woman and she was thrashing around. I could see her dark hair, but I couldn't tell who it was. It was disturbing, and I described it to my husband. I sensed that someone was in trouble and maybe I could help by saying prayers. After a while, it passed. Two years later, when both Marie and I returned to the States, we got together and were telling stories. She began to tell me about the difficult birth of her daughter while they were there. She had been very close to dying. I remembered the day of the vision because it also happened to be my Dad's birthday, October 1st. That was the day her daughter was born, and we were on opposite sides of the earth.

Marie and I both went through divorces. She moved to be near one of her sons in Las Vegas, and I remarried and moved to Florida. We talked a few times over the years but mostly stayed in touch through our sons' friendships. Her son was my son's best man at his wedding in Australia.

As things can happen, we drifted apart until one day I was told that she had died.

Marie … What a blessing it was to have known her.

MIMES

I think Show Biz just simply lusted in my heart. Years later, I decided at the age of forty-eight to put together a Mime Troupe. I had ordered some study tapes and descriptions of what some known mimes had done and fell in love with it. I belonged to a church at that time which encouraged the arts in worship and that seemed an appropriate venue in which to do presentations. Around that time, I had also joined an actual dance class and was learning a few tap and adult ballet moves. I was preparing a new roadshow! I found three adventurous women, designed costumes of black/white striped shirts, with red suspenders, and black pants, white gloves and appropriate mime make-up. Easter was coming in a few months, so I wrote a skit around the agony in the garden of Gethsemane, the betrayal and obedience of Christ and used the Via Delarosa music for the story background. The music was mournful and haunting but seemed perfect. We used red, white and purple scarves to create emotional effects within scenes.

We practiced and practiced. We watched the mime tapes over and over, using the exercises to learn mime techniques. We practiced our craft in front of Senior Citizen groups in nursing homes. Unfortunately, in one case they were all in wheelchairs with various stages of dementia, some tethered to their chairs. Their caretakers used the momentary entertainment provided to take a coffee and cigarette break elsewhere.

We began our performance and soon became mesmerized by the slow determination of the various men and women who began to remove their tethers while others removed their clothing, all without making a single sound. It looked like a scene straight out of a silent zombie movie. They were unbelievable swift in what they were doing! Some were stark naked in what seemed like seconds. I told my friends to keep them from falling because they were beginning to move around the room, and I ran to find their helpers. It was as if the facility had deserted. No sound, no person at desks, no one in the halls. We had been abandoned! I finally found them in a small lunchroom and explained what was happening. I never saw people move so fast. They looked like they were shot out of cannons and were gone instantly. As you can imagine, we left quietly even though the personnel thanked us many times for coming.

Unexpectedly, our mis-matched training methods and efforts were rescued, and a true mime troupe was born.

One of the mimes had a friend visiting who was a 'bonified' Broadway actress, traveling as a one-person, one act, story-telling play about the day of the Crucifixion. We begged, pleaded and threw ourselves on her mercy, asking her to help us knit our efforts and story together. That woman surely will be blessed for what she did for us. I'm not too sure that she was so happy about being cornered because at one point in her trying to pull together the mess that we were, I heard her mutter to herself: "I AM AN ACTRESS! I CAN DO THIS!" What she did was nothing short of miraculous. She showed us how to develop scenes within scenes, how to move, work together, how to disappear when not in the scene by standing with our backs to the audience. How to make a table with one of the scarves.

We really only did one complete performance at one of the local churches, but many people were weeping by the end of it.

I hope that it was because they saw the story we were trying to tell.

Ring Around the Rosie

I had never lived with anyone other than my family until I went away to school. My sister and I had shared a room together until that point, so I was used to living with someone. Even though we did paint a line down the middle of the floor once.

I was going to be living for two years in the same house with a high school friend near the hospital where I would be attending a school of Radiologic Technology in Charlotte, North Carolina. I can still feel the excited anticipation regarding my new circumstances. I definitely was ready to leave home.

The house was one of those lovely old pillared, two story southern homes whose owners rented rooms to women. My friend was already settled in with a fellow x-ray student, and I would share a room with a slightly older woman. I was nineteen, so slightly older meant in her twenties and she was more sophisticated than I was. For instance, my make-up meant only different changes in lipstick colors. Hers were trays and boxes of shadows, liners, bottles, brushes and nail polishes. It was fascinating to watch her dress for work or for dates in the evening. Fortunately, she was one of those sweet-tempered, southern North Carolina women who was generous and easy-going and did not make me feel uncomfortable because of my lack of make-up skills or appearance.

Because we had to walk to school and eventually begin taking night calls, which meant being called out at any hour during the night, we three students decided to look for something closer to the hospital. We found the perfect spot, directly across from the hospital. It was a five-bedroom home, women only, and two bedrooms were available. My two friends took the first floor two-bedroom, and I moved in with someone upstairs who would be leaving in a few weeks after which I could have the room to myself.

"To myself" was an important statement because there were five other women upstairs ... and one bathroom. The amount of arguing, yelling and pillaging that went on was awesome. Because most of our personal accessories were similar, not having the variety we now have, everyone was always missing something that didn't look different from everyone else's. Ownership of hair curlers, (no personal dryers or flat irons back then), hair spray, shampoos and personal items was always an issue of debate and accusation. Fortunately, it never reached a physical point, just verbal disagreements with much shouting and stomping around.

Another issue was snacks. Everyone had their stashes of favorite munchies and they were constantly being raided. It was hard to convict anyone since there was no evidence left. The worst thievery was clothing. What made anyone think they could get away with it in such close circumstances? Items were usually 'borrowed' for an evening out and returned in an overly perfumed, wrinkled state. The owner demanded to know who had taken things from their room. Such a group of innocent stares, all looking at each other in puzzlement. "I'm sure it wasn't you or me," I was so grateful for having the only room with a lock that worked.

I stayed in that rooming house until four of us moved to a small apartment near the hospital for the last six months of our training. I remember very little about the apartment except for the weekend that I came down with the Hong Kong flu which was epidemic that year.

All my roommates just happened to go home that Easter weekend and the owners, who lived downstairs, were also gone. I had weekend call and had to stay in town. All alone, as I slowly realized that I was surely going to meet my demise, with no one to witness it. I was going to die, right there in that little apartment.

The flu started with a fever and cough, then rapidly progressed to getting rid of whatever I had eaten during the past two weeks. After becoming weak, and running back and forth to the bathroom, I simply moved in with a quilt on the floor and prepared to meet my Maker. I wish I had thought to make notes or had written a letter, just some post-script to the world that I had been there. But miraculously, I began to realize I was going to live, and was getting hungry. There was not a scrap to eat in the apartment, so I had to dress and walk four blocks to the hospital to get a meal in the cafeteria. I remember that walk, seeming to take forever, and I wondered if I was going to make it. Years later, I could still see the distance in my mind's eye, a long tree-lined avenue with cars parked and the sun shining.

Forty years later, I visited that same area in Charlotte and saw the apartment again. I could only stand and stare at it in astonishment. It sat only two houses away from the hospital entrance.

Roses Are Red, Violets Are Blue, But ....

Roses are red, violets are blue, but ...... why am I feeling hard, sharp, flat edges? And why am I squashed down on them?

The last thing I remember was the need to grab something that was just out of my reach.

The room is dark, and I hear no sound except someone else's breathing.

I lay there trying to think ... what happened? Did the ceiling fall for some reason? An explosion of some kind? I checked myself ... there is pain in my face, my shoulder and left arm. Can I move? There is something on top of me. I ease myself up in the darkness, and the object on my back falls to the floor. I feel something wet rolling down my face. Am I bleeding? What IS this? I stand up. I walk across a room and find a door. I open it. It's a bathroom. I can see myself in the mirror, in the half light from the outside streetlamp. My face has blood running down it, onto my neck.

I remember only my last thoughts. Was it a terrorist attack?

No, it was a nightmare in which I urgently had to grab an object before anyone else could get to it.

I had launched myself from the bed onto the nightstand.

Epilogue

I dressed, after stopping the obvious bleeding, and went to a 24-hour CVS store to buy butterfly bandages to tape my chin back together. The look on the clerk's face plainly said that 'my purchases were not going to be enough.'

The doctor at Medac decided to use 'surgical crazy glue' on the one-and-a-half-inch gash in my chin. The bruises on my shoulder and arm would heal. My son had to use a hammer and screwdriver to get the nightstand drawer back onto its track. The lamp was still working.

And my dog, apparently, is not disturbed by the sudden violence of things crashing around in a room.

And I wish I could remember what it was that I was trying to grab ....

SECOND STAR ON THE RIGHT

The drive up there was terrifying enough, let alone not knowing what to expect after listening to conversations for ages about this 'new place to live.'

I was in a car with two other women, my friend Jean and her daughter. We had traveled for a couple of hours on a flat, straight road with the early sun shining in on us from the east. The sides of the road were filled with sand, rocks and cactus for as far as we could see, with only road signs and an occasional gas station to break the sterile views. That kind of landscape was unremitting, offering only grade changes of land for a difference of sight. But we were subtlety climbing, which I hadn't noticed until my ears started feeling tight. Suddenly I saw an immense hole in the ground.

It looked like an immature Grand Canyon, with the road meandering in switchbacks down to the bottom and then back up to the rim far on the other side. It looked like a mile down into it! Jean's daughter and I both screamed "Slow down!" at the same time.

But my friend said mildly, "I've traveled here many times. I know what I'm doing."

"Slow down!" we screamed again, while fearing that startling her might cause her to sail off the edge of the road into the depths that we could not see yet.

"Ok, ok," she grudgingly agreed with a crooked grin, regarding the two greenhorns in the car. We both white-knuckled the ride down into the depths and held our breath going back up.

When we could bear to take our eyes off the road, feeling sure we needed to give continual observation to the road ahead and my friend's speed, we found unbelievable beauty all around us.

The early morning sun was developing shadows along the sides and depths of the mountains that were grouped together around the canyon. The mountains were massive and majestic. The landscape constantly changed as we moved around each curve and angle of the road. It looked as if we were on another planet. There was little vegetation, unimaginable color changes, steep, deep ravines and guard rails along the roadside that began to look flimsy.

We finally reached the top of the canyon on the other side, realizing 'we have to do that AGAIN to go home.' At the new mesa elevation, we were near an elevation of 6,000 feet. We had just driven up from a two-foot sea level town where they lived. I noticed a slight change in my breathing pattern, but we were visually on safer footing, flat land. We drove for about another hour, passing through small towns, when my friend mentioned we had just driven across an Apache Indian Reservation while in the canyon.

We finally turned off the main road, going through a small residential community, until we reached the end of the paved road and drove on rutted dirt making several unmarked turns, passing wire fences and gates with open-range steers roaming freely. There were very few buildings, up and down small hills, until she finally said, "We're here."

"We're where?" I asked.

"Here," she said, indicating a large Quonset building with a spiffy-looking trailer beside it, which was going to be our residence while there.

My friend had fallen in love with the idea of living on top of a mesa where the wind blows constantly. The good news was that it did have a working well and she had solar panels that had been installed for the building and the trailer. She was totally 'off the grid' regarding electricity, social services, Emergency Medical Service (they do not leave paved roads, which was a wise decision) and police protection (that was provided by U.S. Marshals when needed). She had chosen not to have a television or computer while there, so her only source of communication was radio, ham radio or cell phone. She kept the phone charged and her car full of gasoline.

Once I got out of the car, I could only stand and turn in circles. It WAS magnificent, in an abandoned planet sort of way. I could see distant mesas and only scrubby vegetation. There were hundreds of animal tracks around the area of her home, including something with huge paws.

We unpacked the car. She had brought pads of bottled water, food, and supplies that she and we were going to need. We had come with her to help rearrange the interior of the building, that was being outfitted with insulation, walls, a kitchen, bath, studio, ham radio room, storage, running water and solar energy. We would stay in the trailer, which was very nice with a kitchen, full bath, heating, dining area and could sleep five. It was the last time my friend would use it herself because it was just for guests.

The interior of the Quonset was generous in size. We moved many things to the storage area. Most of the building already had the interior walls up that were waiting for sheetrock and painting. She had bought a 100-year-old French wood stove for heating and cooking for herself. She had several ingenious ideas such as a sleeping and storage loft. There was a washer, but no dryer because the solar system could not provide that much electricity. She had started a small green house outside with many green plants in it. Neighbors were few and far between and mostly kept to themselves but were readily available for emergencies.

The wind never stopped blowing. The next morning a neighbor stopped by to chat. I asked him, "Does it always blow like this?" He looked thoughtfully off in the distance for a moment and then said "No, sometimes it blows the other way." I asked about the tracks on the ground. The neighbor explained they were deer, huge jack rabbits, small creatures and large pumas' tracks. Needless to say, my friend seldom went outside at night. Her dog was carefully walked and drained before sunset. There are no streetlights. There are no streets. Just the hard dirt ruts that become muddy dirt ruts in the rainy season. Neighbors cheerfully helped each other dig out of the mud and each took the responsibility of carrying large rocks and stones in their cars and trucks to add to the biggest mud holes. That effort helped to ensure that they could pass over them.

I had to stop occasionally to catch my breath, while working, because the altitude was so high, and it was desert country. I definitely was not used to it, coming from a sea level home. When Jean comes to visit me, she sleeps more, not being used to the 80 to 90 percentage of humidity in my air.

I worry about my friend, Jean, living so far out by herself, but she has thrived there. It's been a test of her ingenuity and instincts, for sure, but I think she wouldn't trade the experience for anything.

THE AVON ADVENTURE

There were naked women on the walls. Lots of them. Huge posters of beautifully posed women in many stages of undress. There was also a young man in the room who seemed oblivious to what was around us. He was having a conversation with me regarding prices, scents and samples. I didn't know where to look. So, I concentrated on him.

"What?" I asked.

"These," he said, "I like these. I would like all of them. When will you be back?"

"Next week," I assured him and packed up my samples to leave, wishing he would redecorate between now and then.

I had found him by simply knocking on doors. An act which was intimidating at first but after I realized that different circumstances were behind each door, I found it to be fun, often having unexpected consequences. Definitely a good way to meet new people and provide what appeared to be a happy service for them.

I had just returned from three years of living in England and found myself needing something else to fill my time besides train trips, brass rubbing and learning British bird calls, as I had done while overseas. I also still had a boy at home, too young to start school. I felt the need to find other social avenues and ways to meet new friends and fill the hours between one o'clock and three o'clock when my son was napping.

I know what, I thought, *I'll sell Avon cosmetics.*

It sounded perfect. Something completely different from what I had ever done, and I could arrange my own working hours. I contacted the local representative and made arrangements to pick up my working case with samples, for which I paid a modest price. I was given an area to work in, near my home that didn't conflict with other salespersons' territories. All I had to do was work my way through neighborhood phone lists or knock on apartment doors. A surprising number of people were very accommodating to Avon products and the people who provided them.

I loved the sales meetings where I met many of the other women in my area of town. There were refreshments, sales songs and contests. I once won the fragrance of my choice by being the only one to name all eight scents on cotton balls, arranged in a line on a tray. A proud moment. I don't remember my fellow sales-friends, but I do remember some of my customers.

The most fun were the schoolteachers who had received many of our Avon products from their students at Christmas. They all wanted to exchange them for the products they really wanted the most – usually cosmetics. They had a wonderful time, trying on colors, colognes and samples. There were usually two or three of them, meeting in each other's apartments, with all their products.

One customer was troubling to me. She obviously was being physically abused. I would often see bruises on her, and the two small children would stay very close to her. Sometimes her husband would be there, and it was very uncomfortable to have him in the room. Usually, she managed to make our appointments when he was away, and she would prepare coffee and treats for us. She was obviously a very sweet but lonely and frightened woman. I've remembered her often, over the years, and wondered if she was able to change her circumstances, because she and the children disappeared one day. I have wondered if I would behave differently now, 50 years later, if I met someone having those problems. We have more information and more socially acceptable ways to help them out of their dilemmas.

One of my customers had two huge St. Bernard dogs who would run up and down her stairs in excitement, wagging their big heads back and forth, slinging saliva on the walls and stair rails. How DID she keep her house so clean, I used to wonder? I used to often feel like a Mother Confessor because so many of my customers had problems they simply wanted to speak about. One had just discovered her child had autism. Another had just delivered a child who had Down's Syndrome. I had witnessed her excitement through most of her pregnancy. There were too many to mention who were simply lonely and alone.

Looking back, I consider it as a privilege to have been a part of their lives for a short time. My young child went to kindergarten the next year and I went back to work at a hospital in Baltimore. I understand that most of the Avon sales are through the Internet now. It was a special opportunity to see life up close that now someone now is missing.

SWEETS I HAVE KNOWN

My wedding cake. I had met with the owner of the bakery several weeks before, to discuss how it was to be made and what decorations were to be used. We sat together in her office – she with her pad and pencil and I with my expectations. I told her that it was to be two layers, hopefully small and elegant because I would be taking it to a restaurant for an intimate dinner with friends. I asked that the top layer be a tiny one that my husband and I could share on our first anniversary. She was all smiles and expressed happiness at my occasion and her ability to give me exactly what I wanted. I left, feeling I was in very good hands. It was a simple, but an important need.

I might also mention the wedding bouquet here because it was another item to check off my to-do list. The florist was attentive and at-the-ready with her pad and pencil, furiously writing and drawing my wishes for a small bouquet to reflect the fall season of my marriage. I expressly asked for no bows on seats, or anywhere. And NO eucalyptus in the floral arrangement because I definitely did not want to spend my wedding moment smelling nothing but that strong medicinal effluvium. She assured me she would take care of it, and I distinctly remember her slashing great lines under the words "no eucalyptus!" with her pencil.

The day of the wedding, I was anxious to see the bakery's work. It was perfect. An innocent, charming, delicate little confection with lovely sugar flowers and ribbons with a tiny satin wedding bell surrounded by tiny ribbons and lace on its small top layer. The cake was taken to the restaurant where it charmed everyone with its intricate design and lush icings. I removed the top layer, so we could enjoy the rest of cake, and took it home with us.

My husband and I were to leave that evening for our honeymoon, so I put the cake into the refrigerator for the three days we would be gone. Unfortunately, I had not left any instructions or mention of the cake, while we were away, for the two teenagers who would be in and out of the house.

When we returned, there was a nice-sized slice cut out of one side the cake by my husband's 16-year-old son. "No matter," I thought, "it will just make a charming story to tell later," being grateful that there was still some of it left. I wrapped and boxed the cake to put into our freezer to wait a year for its next appearance.

The day arrived. I had planned a celebration dinner, set the table and brought the cake up from the freezer. I set the box on the counter and lifted the lid. I could immediately see that the wrappings had been removed. There was not a scrap of icing left on the entire cake. My husband's 18-year-old daughter had spent the past year pinching off pieces of the icing when the mood for something sweet had struck her.

I made an appointment with the bakery and explained the circumstances of the wedding cake and ordered just the tiny little top layer to be done again as a surprise for my husband. When I arrived to pick it up, the bakers were beaming with happiness and expectations and all of them had gathered for the presentation. They had baked only the large bottom layer and decorated it for a fare-thee-well.

Oh, and the eucalyptus? My wedding bouquet was filled with the stuff and every aisle seat had a bow on it.

If you have ever made a trip to Britain, you will remember that there is a tea shop on almost every corner of the island. They are filled with every confection, cupcake and goodie known to man. Great piles of them are arranged on plates in the front windows. There are plates of cupcakes shaped as butterflies, crumpets, scones, and jelly-filled pastries. I made a decision then and there that I would try one of each before I left the country. There were mince pies, pink and white Battenberg cakes, Dundee cakes, sponge cakes with marzipan, tarts and scones with clotted cream and raspberry jam, all to delight the eye and sit on plates next to your cup of tea. Four o'clock teatime is a gentle, necessary time in Great Britain. You can feel the need in the air, as natives and tourists look for a shop in which to sit, stretch their legs and have a pot of tea with their favorite cake or pastry. It's a much-needed break. There is sugar and milk for the tea, or perhaps lemon slices. It seems to make no sense to me to do that elsewhere … it's just not the same. The tradition would be missing … the anticipation of a favorite ritual.

Then there are the favorite goodies you try to keep for yourself. That mainly involved hiding them from the three boys who lived with me. Over the years, I had maintained and scouted out many such places. My favorite one was the washing machine. They never went near that. It usually involved my addiction to and affection for chocolates. I seldom have turned down a chance for a piece of cake. I understand the delight pies can generate, but in my generation growing up, the cake reigned supreme. That's where our family's treasured recipes came out and were pressed into service. One haunts me to this day. A neighbor's white, three-layer coconut cake. It was moist beyond belief, a delicate vanilla flavor and icing that was creamy perfection. I had a slice once and hunted for that recipe forever, since she didn't share hers. A memorable stroke of luck brought me her entire cake at a community bake sale. I had just found and paid for it, when the pastor of the church walked up and said "Oh, you've bought it this year." So help me, despite the obvious disappointment in his eyes, I picked it up and took it home. I think I must have thought, "*he has enjoyed it for several years, this one is mine.*" And wonderful the cake was.

Through the years, I've had great favorites: The ice cream cups with wooden spoons, Mother's purloined chocolates and fudge, and many wonderful desserts made all over the world. Let's just say that I never met a sweet I didn't like.

CRIME, BURGLARY, AND PABLUM

Looking back, seven years old can be a very inventive, explorative age. We had just moved to Venice, California during the war and lived in an upstairs apartment. Mother was pregnant again and less able to keep track of me. We were near the ocean, canals, some billboards to climb on and streets where I could ride my new hand-made scooter. The area around our apartment lent itself to a life of discovery, exploring, crime and retributions.

The scooter was my first set of wheels. Dad made it using a dismantled skate and board to stand on. He nailed the skate parts below and added an upright board with handles for a handsome steering column. Life was never the same once I pushed off. A school next door had lots of space to practice wheelies, turns, and offered ample opportunities to speed. Most of my friends had one of these handmade traveling boards, so we were busy with races and simply roaming around. Unfortunately, the canals had no guard rails along the sides of them and sometimes a kid would ride his scooter into the water. As far as I can remember, there was always someone around to jump in and save him or her.

This was the same neighborhood where I learned naughty words and practiced them in chalk on the sidewalks. I can still feel the cement under my knees as I crawled around with a rag and a bucket of water, washing all my sins away. This was also the year I taught classes in lighting matches under an abandoned house with two or three of my friends. I'm not sure who told my Mother, but I do remember the spanking I got. She tucked me between her legs and whacked me with one of her slippers. Truly, I never did light another match. At least, not in Venice.

So, I found a new hobby. Burglary.

I really did like ice cream. And we didn't have it as often as I would have liked. There was always some change on the top of my parent's dresser. I began to take a coin or two from time to time and treat myself to an ice cream bar. I would then climb a huge billboard which was along the street and sit, swinging my legs, as I enjoyed the fruits of my labors. Unfortunately, my sticky fingers expanded their areas of operations. I took some pennies from my parent's friends' home while they were play-ing cards. I put them in the pocket of my dress. When Mother undressed me that night, the pennies fell out. I can still hear that sound as the pennies fell to the floor. I can still consider the silence as both of us looked at the pennies, still rolling and lying around the room.

"Where did you get those?" she asked. And she had THAT LOOK in her eyes. I never liked to tamper with "That Look." Things only got worse.

"I stole them," I admitted.

Mother was always creative with punishment.

In those war years, our sugar came in little white cotton bags with strings attached to pull them shut. Every evening my dad came home and after we had had dinner, the family would stroll along the beach on a boardwalk. My atonement for stealing pennies was to wear one of those bags on both my hands. If anyone asked why they were there, I was to tell them. I was grateful for the people who thought I had been burned, these being bandages, and they had stopped to offer sympathy. I hoped to let that be the reason for both hands being in sacks, but no … there is That Look again.

"No ma'am. I have to wear these because I stole pennies." I do remember that people straightened up from their bent position of pity to look at my parents, nod, and walk on. Embarrassment is a great leveler of bad behavior … along with mortification and humiliation. The golden trinity for raising children.

I wouldn't consider a liking for Pablum as the beginning of a life headed for prison, but I couldn't get the idea of eating some out of my head. Mother had finally come home with our baby brother and later was giving him real food. I tasted the cool, creamy substance and craved it from that moment on. She stored it in the kitchen which sat off a back porch that ran the length of the upper story we lived in. This included my and my sister's bedroom … a convenient little alley along the back of the apartment, but Mother often locked the door here due to my frequent night-time foraging. I decided to wait until my parents were asleep and then sneak along the porch to the kitchen door, which happened to have a broken pane near the floor, just my size. I remember getting down and gently stuffing myself into and through the space. It took a while and trying not to make any noise I found the Pablum and scooped a big handful into my mouth.

Hey. Seven-year olds aren't cooks. Who knew that it had to be mixed with something liquid? I nearly chocked on the dust of it. I couldn't get it out, down or unstuck. There was a bathroom on the way back to my bedroom, so my idea was to get there and wash it out. I tried to crawl back through the same window but got stuck. Stuck in the window with a mouth full of what is now becoming mush. Some angel of mercy had awakened my mother. The kitchen light came on and there she stood.

You know, I think we really understood each other that evening. Her part was finally, fully accepting that this unpredictable child was going to be with her for the next eleven years. And my part was being eternally grateful for her early warning systems.

Vegans

I'm probably going to be stepping on toes here, but I have long tried to understand the art of being a vegan, or the need ... or the ability. It seems like a lot of work. The people I have met who have chosen that way of living and preparing their meals seem to be driven in their efforts to make the changes and quantify their life-long commitment to never eat anything that had a parent.

I'm remembering a neighbor I had years ago who forced her husband to accompany her into that adventure. Although he didn't seem to be that fond of the changes, and rather than argue with someone who was becoming militant about her choices, he quietly followed. My husband and I had tried a few times to have dinners out with them, but they had a very limited list of restaurants that were acceptable to them and were constantly on the hunt for any new vegan restaurant openings. They rushed out to inspect the menus, always on the quest for newer ways to have vegetables prepared in a more exciting way than they had found by then. I think they were bored and had a significant amount of food fatigue, basically from eating the same things too often. I was not comfortable with her need to grill, question and require lengthy explanations. She researched how and why each preparation was done, making sure that anything containing unacceptable ingredients were not included or were exchanged for something more to her liking.

I haven't noticed that those eating differences have made them healthier or happier than the average person. In fact, vegans can often seem to be harassed or tense a good bit of the time. They seem to be perpetually optimistic about finding new combinations or flavors that will make them happy again.

I had one friend who decided on her own that she would become a vegan. She had no earthly idea how to do that and as far as I was able to determine, she never actually studied or read very much about the mechanics of the completely new world. She just made up her own rules as she went along. I once saw her almost verbally wrestle a waiter almost to his knees, trying to bully him into bringing her a simple bowl of fruit. A large bowl of fruit. My husband I had offered to take her and her husband to a well-known restaurant in their hometown to celebrate our being together after a long separation. The chef was known nationally for his ingenious and delicious preparations. His menu required one to read, study and enjoy its creations in print, let alone, enjoy on a plate.

My friend was suspiciously quiet during our study of the menu as the three of us were comparing notes and enjoying verbal descriptions of the entrées, discussing choices, choosing one then dropping it as we skipped ahead to the next fantasy in the making. What we discovered was, she had already decided to force them to bring her that bowl of fruit. She was not going to even read the menu. She did not want to have to maneuver through the words to find the few items she would allow on her plate.

I remember the waiter trying to be as accommodating as he could be, making simple suggestions regarding some of the specialties and making minor adjustments. She could only envision the horror of not being able to have 'the familiar' brought to her. His final remark to her was that the restaurant had no way to price 'a bowl of fruit.' So, she just sat there as we three tried to enjoy the truly wonderful meals that we had ordered. We tipped very well that evening.

That same friend began to try to understand veganism, but only under her own terms. She studied some fruits and vegetables, but only for their health-aiding properties, for instance, kale is a good source of calcium. She ate so much of it that she began to grow bone spurs. It seemed to me that her only understanding of protein sources were beans. Because she allowed no dairy, eggs or fish of any kind in her diet, she was sorely lacking in protein and developed medically related problems. She included so much flax in her meals, without understanding that it was a natural blood-thinner, a surgeon had a problem stopping the bleeding during a surgery she had done. Who knows what harm she has done to herself from lack of knowledge?

The last time she came to visit, she commented on my choice of foods which included mixtures of meat, vegetables, pastas, grains, salads and fruits. "You don't eat many greens, do you?"

"Yes, just not by the bushel." I responded.

I've had relatives come to visit, for whom I have cooked many meals. I often cook ahead so that I can spend more time with them. Then, they arrive and announce, "I've become a vegan since we met last." Well, thanks for letting me know ahead of time since I've already stocked my fridge. What I later became aware of was that they were not vegans at all, but quasi-vegetarians, and were using it as a dieting tool.

I do admire a True Vegan. They have studied the interactions of the allotted foods and understand what their bodies need to replace the items they have given up. What they do makes sense. They are usually healthy, are glowing and have a lot of energy.

But I've realized I must hurry past their Facebook entries with pictures and commentary about the practices of animal butchery and cruelty.

Either that, or I may never be able to eat meat again.

My Mother Got Run Over
By A Golf Cart

My friend and I were walking our dogs in rainy, dreary English-type weather in Florida chatting about whatever, a dog's health, the color of dog poop in regard to health issues or the latest festivities in town. You know, the usual stuff, while waiting for our dogs to do their business.

We met up with another dog-walker and chatted for a bit, during when she mentioned her lawn had been run over several times by a neighbor that has been making left turns across it. That led to a description of the culprit, who we mentioned had eye surgery not too long ago. That led to the revelation of another event in which the speaker's mother had been run over recently by the lawn perpetrator's golf cart. After or before eye surgery was yet to be determined.

Apparently, the golf cart had knocked her down and then ran over the leg of her eighty-one-year old mother. Now, that could have been serious. Most of us have legs in the sixty-five to eighty-five-year-old range, and we might not have done so well as that lady, who was able to get up and continue walking.

The daughter did not take this lying down. She had immediately composed a song satirizing the event, circumstances and general attitude towards this attack on her mother by the person who had already left tire tracks on her lawn.

Now, I had met this lovely woman several times and had gotten to know her through chats during other dog walks. She had remarkable accomplishments, among which I now must add songwriting in the Johnny Cash genre to the list. That was a delicious realization. She sang a few lines for us a couple of times, which were genuinely funny and obviously enjoyed by herself, myself included. I mean, you don't run into original balladeers every day.

Now, my first friend had a more serious mindset. She kept her conversation tracking on a likely health issue following her elderly legs run over by a golf cart, with memories of an acquaintance who had had similar circumstances and not fared so well. That person received surgery, rehab and was not able to play golf again. No amount of singing or admiration for the lyrics could convince her that the 'mom' was OK and that now we could focus on the joy of celebrating the event in song.

Walking on one side of me was one who wanted social justice and safety on the golf-courses. On the other side, was one who had written and was singing about the event of 'you ran over my mother with your golf cart.' Who gets attention at that point? I have to admit, I sided with the singer at the moment, admiring that new side of her many talents. We both laughed at the sheer fun of what she had done.

We all soon parted, taking our dogs home. My first friend continued her thoughts about what she would be doing that day, never acknowledging what we both had witnessed, a rare revelation of another's ability to knock your socks off, simply with fun.

Visual Harmony

I've watched them, myself unseen, for months. Not deliberately, but mostly chance glances out my windows or while sitting at my desk writing or paying bills. They bring a slow-down of my attention because they always seem to be in a tandem of harmony in whatever they are doing around their home.

They moved into the house across the road about a year ago. Both are tall, graceful people who happen to also be the owner of a large cat that I occasionally see sitting in the sun, just inside their front glass door. From the first, I have thought 'these are not your every-day home-folks.' They have an air of uniqueness about them.

We became more acquainted during one of our occasional hurricanes. The man was still living in and out of town, finishing his time with his company before physically moving to Wilmington, while she moved into their home that was being renovated in many ways and areas. Just about the time he was to arrive to his home, after a visit here, a hurricane decided to definitely head this way.

I asked my new lady neighbor, "Have you ever been in a hurricane before?"

"Not really," being a cosmopolitan D.C. kind of girl.

"Then I am afraid I am the bearer of sad tidings. There are many things that need to be done ahead of time," I said and rattled some of them off for her.

Welcome to a Southern neighborhood, prone to occasional hurricanes.

I'm guessing she called her husband somewhere between here and wherever he was at the time, because he was back the next day. I have to say, that guy's points went way up in my book. I mentioned this to him later and he said, "Yeah, like she's going to let me back into the house if I head on out of the state, telling her to let me know when it's safe to return."

I assume they gathered all the usual information about readying for a storm around here, including the filling of the tubs, stocking up on supplies should the electricity be out for a while AND getting them before the grocery store shelves were cleared. Plus, all the other duties we who have lived here for twenty-plus years have learned. I didn't have time to add a lot more to her chances of coming out of the storm better prepared because I also needed to do the same things, load up the car and leave for safer places, which happened to be Greenville, North Carolina. I decided a long time ago that it just wasn't fun to stay in the house and listen to the shingles flying off and possibly see the trees and walls falling down.

We had another great bonding moment when she called me the next morning to say, "A tree had fallen onto the front of your house. A second one had fallen on top of the security fence that surrounds the community by the side of your house."

Both trees took out most of the landscaping I had just installed about six months before. She asked who might have a key to my home, and her husband offered to get inside to take a look at any damage. Blessings come in many ways. That was one of them. He and another neighbor managed to get to the front door, because the tree limbs were blocking everything and were into my attic. They sawed off the limbs sticking through the roof and sprayed foam into the holes. They also moved most of what was in my master bedroom closet to safer places because the rain was pouring through the space where my ceiling fan used to be. I believe they literally saved my home from a huge amount of destruction. They helped me through many phone calls to find a tree service that was able to remove the trees, cut them up and pile them one-story high in the front of my yard. All of that was taken care of before I was able to return home.

But … back to harmony. I've watched them come out in the early mornings in their pajamas with cups of coffee, standing side by side, surveying their kingdom. Then later coming out together, to dig, plant, weed and drag bags of topsoil around to feed their new plants. Often one is seen washing their car and the other putting new plants in the ground. When they are finished, they may get their Vespa scooter out for a tandem spin around the neighborhood. They are newly retired, and it looks happy over there.

Is that a rainbow I just saw?

Welcome to Wilmington

I have been a knitter, crocheter, and a needle pointer since I was about nine years old. I have always loved the colors and textures of yarns and the intrigue of patterns. There is something wonderfully anticipatory about deciding it's time to make something new and looking for the necessary materials. I have seen such wonderful examples over the years of other's interpretation of stitches and ideas and have copied them or interpreted them in my own way.

There were always baby needs for each child as I had them, including caps, booties, and blankets. I also made those items for friends. My husband's grandchildren began to expect a new set for each child that came along. One of my most memorable adventures was learning to make Alaskan sweaters in Anchorage, Alaska. They contained extraordinary patterns depicting bears, trees, Alaskan totem images, Indian symbols and things native to Alaska. The yarn was the heaviest I had ever used, and I became more skilled at learning to sew seams. I made one for my husband and one for our three-year-old son.

I have bought yarns and patterns from all over the world. England was the most satisfying because every woman in the country was working on something. Yarn shops were delightful with local yarns and hand-dyed materials. The British had years of developing the most unusual and beautiful patterns, and they were everywhere to buy. I was in knitting and needle-pointing heaven.

When my husband and I were considering moving to Wilmington, the very last thing I did was to ask him to pull the car over before we left town so that I could look at a phone book to see if there was a yarn shop in the town, there was. I then told him, "We can move here".

A few years ago, a woman opened a new yarn shop in Wilmington. I stopped in to see what items it might contain. She had moved from another state after her husband had passed and had brought her established shop with her. She did have an extraordinary inventory, but she seemed to be having trouble arranging the items and establishing areas around the rooms in the shop. She had more to offer than another shop in Wilmington, but it was hard to find anything because she was so unorganized. It seemed hard for her to even establish prices. She had magnificent examples hanging around the walls that she had worked herself to show customers how something would look when finished. I stopped in a few more times, and she seemed even more disorganized and unhappier than before.

The last time I stopped by was to buy yarn and the pattern for a wonderful embroidery piece she had displayed in the shop. I said I had come to see the example again and get what was needed to make it. Her face just crumpled. "It's been stolen," she said. "In fact, many of my examples are gone as well as yarns, and knitting accessories are missing." Apparently, customers were taking advantage of her shop having individual rooms, and her inability to see them all the time. They were helping themselves to her stock and simply stealing things.

I felt so sorry for her, as she burst out crying and saying that she was just going to pack it all up and move back to her former home. Shortly afterward, that's exactly what she did.

I have thought about her often over the years and felt ashamed of Wilmington for treating her like that and taking advantage of her struggle to begin again, or for not welcoming her to this town in a good way. I probably knew most of the knitters and sewers in town, because I belonged to several of the guilds and organizations over the years. I can't imagine any of them doing such a thing, but I guess you never know. Apparently, there were many of them with the same idea, because so many things were missing. Her inventory could easily be replaced, but not the pieces she had spent years making.

I don't remember her name, but have wished her well when she would cross my mind. Hopefully, she was able to begin again, somewhere else with kinder customers.

CARE

I thought about it again, as I drove past a building that seemed to be a strange combination of architecture and land-scaping. *What IS that?*, I always thought. The building had an official simplicity, plain and business-like in the front. In the rear of the building, there was a playground including rides, swings and toys surrounded by a high chain-linked fence ... with razor wire coiled around the top. I didn't give it more attention than that – it seemed just an unusual collection of outdoor visuals, as I drove by it each time and wondered why it looked that way.

I had a friend I occasionally met for lunches who had an interesting job. She worked mostly nights manning hot lines at a suicide prevention facility in the same town. Or so I thought. Of course, we never discussed her work or the calls, even though I was thoroughly curious. We were both part of a Christian Mime group I had created, so we had many other conversational areas to explore.

One day she asked me if I might be interested in coming to her place of employment because a seminar was being offered to recruit volunteers for a special need and she thought I might be someone who would fit in. That seemed too intriguing to miss ... especially when I realized that the meeting was being held in the building with the razor wire.

We had to be identified as expected visitors before we were allowed into the building. It was done through an opening that resembled one you might buy movie tickets through. Only, this small opening had bullet-proof glass in it with a lower opening to slide IDs under. Once inside, we were greeted and led into a small room where about five other women were waiting. There was coffee and pastries arranged on a corner tablet that also included workbooks.

What IS this place? I kept asking myself. It looked like a small school entrance inside and I could hear children playing somewhere. I was about to find out.

"Welcome to CARE," said the speaker and coordinator for the event. "CARE stands for the Center for Abuse and Rape Emergencies. You have been invited to visit with us and hear what we are about to say, so you might consider becoming a volunteer here." She then began to give an explanation about what would become a very important episode in my life.

"This organization was created to provide a safe haven, emergency shelter, and to ensure their interests were represented and rights upheld for women and their families who have become victims of domestic violence, sexual assault, homicide and other violent crimes. We offer a twenty-four-hour hotline, free emergency shelter, help for victims to leave unsafe environments safely, victim advocacy, counseling, crisis teams to accompany assault victims and survivors to hospital emergency rooms, community education and much, much more."

I signed up for the three-day workshop followed by an extensive online course. I would begin my instructions to become a volunteer with what would be an intensive, world-cracking, humbling, often terrifying, and deeply satisfying tour of duty with CARE.

The interior facilities were made to seem as home-like as possible, with many hand-made items for children such as quilts and toys, all provided by the generosity of local women. These efforts would help them settle into strange surroundings after having fled their dangerous homes. There were separate bedrooms provided for the mothers and their children, counseling rooms, a wonderful kitchen, play areas and that wide, spacious back yard with the slides and razor wire.

I was quickly indoctrinated into the routine of answering the twenty-four-hour crisis hotlines. There was always a superior there to answer my questions and keep an eye on the families and calls. I was taught how to help callers safely prepare to leave their homes of violence, how to gather small amounts of money and hide it, collect clothing and necessities with which to leave, how and when to leave, and how to let the CARE organization and the local police help them do these things safely. Many nights families were secretly brought through the doors. Soon after, there would often be a man angrily yelling outside and banging on the doors, demanding to be let in, or have the victims returned to him. We always avoided the fact that anyone was there.

After those families were admitted, we would begin with days of counseling which often involved the volunteers, teaching the victims that they had a right to feel safe and be treated well. The CARE advocacy provided support and referral services to ensure victims' rights were protected and fulfilled. We interacted with the children, aware of the traumas they had suffered, too. It was wonderful to see many of them become the little children they were. Unfortunately, others were too angry or hurt to do that.

One of the most interesting activities that CARE sponsored while I was there, was to promote The Clothesline Project. For that, they bought hundreds of white T-shirts, paints, scissors, glue, decorating items, and invited anyone who wanted to participate and make a statement about domestic violence to come and prepare one of the shirts. It was heart-breaking, hilarious, and sobering to see what most of the women and men did to those shirts. Some of them wrote entire stories on them. Others ripped, tore, and stained them as if with blood, all the while crying and shouting about what they had been through. Another cut slits and stabbed all over the shirt and then sewed the openings back together, writing, "You will never hurt me again." Others wrote names on them and then ripped them to hanging shreds. When finished, they were hung in a town square on clotheslines where the public was invited to come and see what had been done. It was incredibly moving. I saw many people walking around crying as they read the shirts. It was hard not to. So many shirts, so much harm done. Possibly there was some healing.

One evening I was manning the hotline. Because it was quiet with few calls and a new family had just come in, I offered to hold one of the babies. The phone rang. It was someone contemplating suicide. I began speaking to a man as we had been taught to do, while holding the phone in one hand and the baby on my lap. I was wildly trying to signal to someone to take the baby without making any noise. I finally held the phone away and whispered loudly, "Suicide!" Someone immediately ran to get one of the managers who came and gently took the baby from my lap. I was able to continue the conversation with a troubled person to a good conclusion.

Calls were seldom easy. Most had to do with someone just having been beaten or wanting advice as to how to get away from the ones who were assaulting them. Sometimes we went to the hospital to be with the victims of rape while they were treated.

One day the police department called to ask if CARE could send over some people to play the "bad guys" during one course of their training. Another volunteer and I went. We were supposed to be resisting arrest while the police were dealing with the situation. We decided we were going to be real tough guys and make it hard for them to do anything with us. I will be forever in awe of how fast they had us pinned to a car with handcuffs slapped on our wrists! I definitely had more respect for their quick decisions and moves after that experience.

It will always be incredible to me, the amount of time, planning, involvement and training that went into doing the work those people had committed to. It wasn't easy, but the results were life changing, for both the managers and volunteers, as well as the thousands of people they helped to a new, safer life.

I Just Can't Take
Me Anywhere

I had been invited to a wonderful experience, a Valentine's Day luncheon, hosted by a friend's mother. Beautiful Valentine creations hung outside on the two front doors and a glass of champagne greeted guests as they entered the elegantly decorated foyer enhanced with delicate lighted arrangements in pots on the floor. The champagnes were in long, beautiful painted flutes.

Several friends were near the foyer, happily chatting and came over to greet me. Somewhere in the hugs, I managed to spill half of my champagne down one hand and sweater sleeve. *No matter, it's colorless,* I thought. *And no one saw it happen.*

The guests and I walked into a beautiful room where we could see the Intercoastal Waterway and a table set for us with a huge bouquet of red and white roses in the center. There were lovely dishes stacked on chargers at our places to hold our feast. Our host created gifts for each of us and Valentine-decorated bags placed in front of our seats. With charming Brandenburg-lace placemats under it all, a red organza napkin for our laps as well as a decorated paper napkin for our gentle clean-ups, our hosts created a festive table.

Let the fun begin, I thought.

The first course was a luscious tomato bisque soup with a heart-shaped grilled cheese sandwich and a rolladin of tender chicken breast with prosciutto ham wrapped around it. The soup bowl was a heavy clear green glass. In all the chatting back and forth and while leaning forward to see each other, my soup bowl tipped and poured about half of the liquid down the front of my ruffled shirt and slacks. I quietly mopped up what I could with the paper napkin, but there was still quite a bit left. No one had noticed the clean-up going on, because of the lively conversation taking place. I tried to unobtrusively get the heart-decorated dishcloth out of my gift bag. Little did I know there were wrapped, round chocolates stuffed on top of it. The bright colored chocolates rolled around the table, and some fell on the floor. In the meantime, I was still busy quietly mopping. Friends were chasing candies and still chatting. I eased the cloth out of the bag, and it did a much better job than the now sodden paper napkin. A crisis was soon passed.

As the third course arrived, I observed a magnificent heart-shaped chocolate cylinder in a dish of ice cream. It was in a delicate crystal dish. We all gently knocked on the chocolate, fearful of breaking the dish if we pushed too hard. "How do we eat this?" my friend asked her daughter. "That's for you to figure out," she said. The table came alive with suggestions and attempts to break into it. My friend managed to break off a piece. "Delicious!" she crows. By that time, we all managed to eat the ice cream and were talking about taking the cylinder home. I decide to put mine into my fresh cup of coffee. Bingo!

It was perfect. Coffee mocha compliments of a home-made treat ... and I had a chocolate mustache to show for it.

Another time I tried to dodge a mishap without anyone noticing happened when I set myself on fire. I DO hate to make a scene. That was back in the years when I would light a cigarette at gatherings. We had gone out for the evening and I was wearing a long skirt. Apparently, the cigarette ash had gotten longer than I usually allowed, and it pulled some of the embers down into my lap when it fell, unnoticed. I quickly had my very own small campfire going. I squeezed my skirt and slip together in a hot little wad and held it until the fire seemed to have gone out. I looked around and no one had noticed my quiet struggle. When I stood, there was a large hole burned through the fabric. Still no one noticed. Not even the odor of burnt fabric. It was another success.

Those kinds of mishaps started at an early age. I missed going to see the very first Disney Snow White movie because I had spilled chocolate on the front of my best dress without telling Mother, so she could clean it. And there was always the chunk of spinach in one's teeth the entire evening or mascara that has wilted down onto your cheeks during the day. And dare we say the words, "nasal issues"? It happens to everyone.

You've got to love the events you catch others in. My husband and another couple knew someone who had made their own home-brewed beer. We stopped by to check it out before going on to London, to a British garden party. The other wife and I did not care for beer so a kind twist of fate in the universe saved her and me from later public humiliation. We arrived at the afternoon party and my husband and his friend suddenly started foaming at the mouth. They couldn't stop it or control it. It just kept foaming out. They stood looking at each other, with panic and disbelief. The foam just kept rolling out. They tried drinking something but that only made it worse. My friend and I were hysterical at the sight of our helpless husbands bubbling over. The four of us made apologies and escaped before our husbands became public viewing interests and wound up on the BBC evening news.

I apparently have a tendency to get involved in other's food problems. I was out one evening with a friend who had worn a beautiful crepe silk blouse. She spilled red wine copiously down the front. She tactfully asked me to find a bottle of soda and then sponge the red spot with the soda. I suggested we retire to the ladies' room, but she was adamant. It was to be a public spectacle, although her back was to the room, and besides, "Red wine sets very fast," she said. So, I am scrubbing away with a napkin and the soda and begin to realize my friend has a very firm bosom. A little helpful surgery? I eventually did a good job. She was right, soda will remedy red wine. It's part of the wisdom of age.

I probably do need a drop cloth when I eat. I tend to litter tables when the food falls off my plate as I shred and search for favorite pieces to eat. There seems to always be a messy plate with debris left that were once a culinary presentation. I am definitely not a member of the Clean Plate Club. Unless there is a dessert coming. A plate full of food just makes me want to separate and create other combinations of food, especially if I don't like what is there or there is too much of everything. It leads to equal splashes, drips, splatters and sticky fingers as I entertain myself while chatting. There are a few faithful friends who have noticed my messy way of eating and still ask me to lunch. I usually avoid salads, they just take too long to search, identify and separate. Just last night at a restaurant, I was trying to slide some of the communal butter onto my bread plate. As usual, the warmer knife helped the butter slide off onto the table. No paper napkins or even a paper coaster available to help it. I waited until the table attention slid away from my activities to another focus, and so help me, I found that a paper sugar packet can be a tiny help in scraping up buttery messes. God forbid that someone should give me something shattery, like a croissant, because it's going to explode into the air like Fourth of July fireworks the instant I bite into it, usually sticking around one's mouth like funky little cat whiskers. I have discovered a little trick that works though. If I hum or sing while carrying something liquid, it tends to stay in the cup. Bless the person who invented saucers to catch those sloshing liquids.

Once in a while, everyone has had to walk around part of a day with blots of food or drink on their shirts. A subtle, visual confession of bad aims, leaky forks, or just plain fun with food. How DO those people swiftly eat their meals, lay their forks down on a clean plate and have time left over to watch me stack, move food around and munch on good finds? They will never know what they are missing.

THE LIFE OF A STUDIO CORKBOARD

The oldest thing on it is a pencil sketch of a photo of myself, taken when I was around five years old. I think I was in the fourth grade when I drew it. It's a tolerable likeness. The page is from a small notebook my dad kept, and the unlined paper is about seven inches by three-and-a-half inches. All of that makes the drawing around seventy-four years old. How it has been kept this long can only be a mystery. I can mention that on the same wall is hanging a framed oil I did about the same year. It would make you think of something from a Walt Disney movie. It was more evidence that I often would get into Mother's art materials ... and for some reason she kept what I had done.

Right above that piece is a school picture of my first great love. He's sixteen and reminds me of a dark-haired Leslie Howard, Scarlett O'Hara's heartthrob in the movie, *Gone with the Wind*. It's signed "Love always, Glenn," above his head. Unfortunately, his parents moved away and took him with them. He wasn't much of a writer, so our friendship couldn't be sustained. I have often wondered where he is today and how many other times, he might have signed something, "Love always."

In the middle of the board is a photo of four pairs of booted, denimed legs. I love that picture for some reason. I've kept it hanging wherever I am for thirty-two years. They are the legs of my three sons and one of their wives. I painted a watercolor of it once and gave it to the oldest boy. I suspect his wife kept it after his divorce a few years ago.

There are happy times pictured above that one—the three boys happily munching grilled chicken in an English outdoor pub garden. They actually look very British there with pale skins, bushy hair styles of the early '70s, and gangly young teenager looks. The youngest is about four and an adorable curly haired blond. He finally began to not notice the hands that would come out of the British crowds on the sidewalks and unbidden, run their fingers through his hair. A tribute to cuteness, anonymously passing by.

Ah … there are the three of them, as young men, mustachioed, bearded and looking like fugitives from a Latino chain-gang, having just escaped from crushing rocks on a mountain road. They are trim, have short haircuts (finally), suntanned and big smiles on their sweet faces. In this one, they are all about the same height. A testimony to their individual growing rates.

There is some artwork represented. One is a photo of a ceiling height, life-sized oil painting Mother did in the corner of the hallway, outside mine and my sister's bedroom door. It's of Jesus in the temple with the wisemen. That one is now puzzling since at the time Mother was an undeclared Jew. It's either a religious cross-over or a blending of Christianity and Judaism for her. Was she subliminally declaring herself to us? This did not become the mystery it is until now, since she died at forty-eight and I didn't learn of her background until I was much older. Mother was always full of surprises even after she was gone.

Another piece of art is a copy of the home-page artwork for a website I used to have, called Floorcloths and More.com. It's of a three foot by six foot acrylic wall-hanging painting of an oriental styled crane standing in a pool, with Art Nouveau bamboo and floral decorations around it. I had the website for a number of years when I was painting and selling paint-ed canvas rugs. I also added pillows and wall hangings to my inventory. Those are busy memories.

There are odds and ends of other things push-pinned to the board: various pictures of my sister and I, samples of fellow artist's abstracts, favorite cartoons, a painting color chart and a piece of poetry one of my sons had written:

The comfort of memories,
Childhood dreams and maturity.
Sunbeams of the soul,
Gaining ever love.

A course of time,
Directing the answers.
The strength of love,
Maintaining the heart.

Hanging in one corner, as a tribute to some painted China pieces I had submitted to the Anne Arundel County Fair in Annapolis, Maryland, is a purple First Prize ribbon. A little corner of bragging rights.

A separate, favorite art piece, hanging above the cork board holds multiple pieces of a cut-up painting, reassembled to create an abstract art. Attached to the board is a card which says on the front and written beside a multi-colored cat:

> "I am Me. I am just Me.
> I am a little like other cats,
> But mostly I am just ME."

This seems like a good ending.

Up and Down the Street

We all normally live on streets with neighbors. Some we remember and some we don't. Over the years, I had one group of neighbors whose memories have stayed with me. They seemed the perfect matching sets, complimenting each other in their own unique ways. They were an unusual variety.

Directly across the street was Dottie. She seemed to be the organizer, mother confessor and most sympathetic person on the street. She was the first to offer any help in any way, made extra money by baby-sitting other's young ones and was also the nosiest and gossipiest of the neighborhood. It was understood that if you were available each morning after children had left for school, coffee klatches were held in her enclosed garage. Often mothers would stroll down, still in their robes and holding their coffee cups. I was a working mom, so I never joined that sisterhood. Dottie and her husband were an Italian variety, small, friendly, and out-going. Their eight-year-old boy was beautiful and able to run so fast that I used to wonder if he had air in his bones.

Next door to Dottie was the Dragon Lady. Most of the neighborhood kept a slight distance from her and small children were afraid of her. Her husband, whom few had ever seen, had lived with the Dragon Lady on the street the longest. She often would stand outside with her arms akimbo to glare and patrol her lawn. No one was allowed to step on her grass. The kids used to taunt her by standing on the little strip of grass along the street, declaring that it was public property until she would walk toward them and then they would run. Dottie seemed to be the only one who could get close to the Dragon Lady and managed to encourage her to attend the coffee klatches. Dragon Lady liked having the neighborhood news reports apparently, but not enough to get them from individuals. Group therapy was more to her liking.

Two doors down from her was the neighborhood beauty, also Italian but about six feet tall with the posture of a model. That was Marie. She had a problem with agoraphobia, a fear of going out in public alone. Marie's answer to that dilemma was to make her home one of the most comforting, fun and interesting ones on the block to visit in. It was always filled with new ideas and plenty of baked goods to munch on. She became my best friend on the street. I loved her creativeness and adventurism. As long as someone was with her, she would do anything. The first time we went somewhere together we had our four boys sitting in the back seat. As we drove away, her oldest said, "Miss Diane, this is the first time my mom has been out in someone else's car." There was deadly silence in the car and a tight look on his mom's face. Marie had once found a hairdresser who worked from her home (Marie's answer to not having to go to a public salon), and she invited me to go along with her. We both got such glamorous hair styles that we convinced our husbands that they should take us out that night.

Across the street from Marie, for a time, was a couple with four children who had problems ... big problems. The wife was a sweet lady whose husband was a raging alcoholic. He once smeared her clothes with peanut butter, cut them up and threw them out the window of their second story. I once caught his oldest boy chasing my two sons with a butcher knife. Police were often called by the wife. We all were sympathetic, but those were dangerous situations, and we were all fearful of what might be going on inside the house. I wish I had good news about them, but they moved after a short time and were replaced by an Army Colonel, his wife and their four children. The husband wore the officer's insignia, but she was the officer in the family. Their children were subdued but delightful. He was seldom seen, but pleasant. Once she invited me to come for coffee, but I explained that I worked and wasn't available right then. She waited until my car was home one morning and sent one of the children over with a note, and in it "she 'commanded' me to come to her house. "Right now!" I thanked her for the invitation but explained that it wasn't possible just then. I had been teaching one of her daughters how to sew at the time, and after that occurred, she would no longer let the child come to my home or speak to me. They moved shortly after that, but her husband knocked on my door before driving away and said, "I need to ask, why didn't you ever come to visit my wife?" I told him what had happened. He just looked sad and left. I kind of think that it wasn't the first time they had to move, due to circumstances and possibly it was why they didn't live in base quarters.

Next door to us was a quiet husband and wife. I worried that my two grammar schoolboys and Dachshund were noisier than they would prefer, but they never indicated that they were and always offered a friendly wave when we saw each other, even after my youngest had dug up all of her daffodil bulbs one time, thinking he was harvesting onions. After work, the husband usually sat outside in back, in the shade of his only tree, with his newspapers. Our bonding moment occurred one day when my dog escaped our backyard and turned over a trash can to eat as much as she could stuff in and waddled back home with a protruding tummy. She had done that before and my frustrated husband picked her up, took the lid off our trash can and dropped her into it. The neighbor sitting next door under the tree almost fell off his chair laughing so hard. He and my husband were best friends from that day. I think he considered any man that would throw his dog into the trash can was OK with him.

Around the corner only a block or so away was the Scottish wife of a young Navy man. Unfortunately, he had a drinking problem and was less than kind to her. Once she showed up with a black eye. They had three small children (bairns, she called them) and having met her before, she would often wander around to my house, knocking on the door to ask, "Deeann (she called me in her Scottish lilt), yee got anyee scandal?" looking for some coffee and a few minutes to chat. I hope that our few times together afforded her a chance to feel like a normal mom with friends 'just down the street.'

Even though those women were all very different, they interacted with each other in good, caring ways. Even though we saw and understood each other's trials, most of the time, it didn't affect how we ultimately cared for each other.

A Sum of the Parts

I am in a jail … of sorts. I have not been given a release date and I do not have normal visiting privileges. I don't even know *why* I am here. Yes, I realize there is a world-wide pandemic, but WHY am I here? There was no formal sentencing, no list of accusations, no accusers. Life just seems to have flowed into this space along with millions and millions of other people. This feels like false imprisonment with no time of release or time off for good behavior. And you know what? I don't like it.

It's very comfortable here, by most jail standards. I have most of what I need. It does have a threat, though, along with these circumstances. This threat appears in notices that are constantly changing in the newspapers, television and conversations with friends. And there is no way to accurately judge what is going on because it keeps changing daily around the world. The promise of harm to each of us is real and up close if we do something foolish and unintended. It's like having a stalker that is daring you to not follow the rules or make a misstep.

Four months ago, I didn't have to plan for escapes in all that I would do. I didn't have to carefully plot out my travel route, how to approach people or doorways, and what must be done before entering or leaving while there. And then to worry once you return to your living space about whether you had done everything right and if you had escaped the stalker once again. And so, you wait for further bulletins.

We constantly compare notes with friends and neighbors about how and what we do now. Is this a safe distance from you? Why aren't you wearing your mask today? We now know how far our spit travels when we speak or cough. We all have become more proficient at shopping online and keeping an eye out for items that we are going to need as our supplies diminish. My friends have become efficient at sewing masks but the criteria for how safe they are, or not, also keeps changing. Heaven forbid that one would need unusual care such as a dentist or a doctor. How in the world is one going to plan that from beginning to end? It's a battle strategy now.

It's hard to really imagine this being repeated all over our world, even when we have the images on television showing us the devastation that many are facing and have faced. The numbers that are daily posted, the mass graves being shown are astonishing in their reality.

And yet, life is trying to go on. Everyone wants to be 'normal' again but is it too soon? How is this judged? And what is the *new* normal going to be? The world has lost itself in so many ways during this pandemic time. Many are learning they can work from their homes, do without and are learning new ideas of sharing with each other. There seems to be a desperate need to get outdoors into the sunshine, even to the tossing off of all safety measures and mingling with hundreds of others on beaches and parks. How foolish could this appear if many more have been exposed to the stalker because of their personal negligence. We do have choices we can make and now can only hope that they are the right ones.

It's All Relative

It's no use going back to
yesterday, because I was a
different person then.
Lewis Carroll

HER MOTHER'S FACE

It was strange sitting across from her in a western Florida restaurant. We had not seen each other for almost twenty years, and before then, it had been forty years. Even before, I had only the image of her in a photo in which she was about five years old, riding a rocking horse, having the ringlets, coloring and dimpled cheeks of a Shirley Temple.

Now I see her mother's face when her mother was about 65, with the same Jackie-Kennedy-whispery-breathy voice and speed-talking staccato that her mother had, along with the love of historical descriptions that they both collected and had at the ready for lengthy discourses at all times. Fortunately for both of them, they were entertaining and had a wonderful vocabulary of adjectives with which to describe the family scenarios they had gathered over the years. My cousin had now become the family caretaker of all familial information.

That all began when I needed to make a quick trip to Florida to check on my aging and ailing brother. My cousin lived about four hours from there, and I would have time to leave early enough to spend an afternoon with her on the way back to North Carolina. One phone call worked out the time and logistics of getting together. I collected all of the old photos and memories I had to show her, and she planned to do the same for me.

She and I had spent all those years missing each other, because she lived in Ohio most of her life and I had spent mine moving endlessly between Alaska, England and points in-between. I always thought my life was rich within its expansions and travel, but I found hers was rich interiorly, filled with the family linages.

We arrived at a quiet restaurant with our packages of letters and photos. I've since wondered what her first impression of me was, but never thought to ask because I was too busy analyzing her visual lineage for myself. She did have an amazing likeness to her mother, even while aging, and the same vocal self-assuredness of her mother. After exchanging bulletins of the health and welfare of our mutual sides of the family, we began to remove our paper memories from the bundles we had brought. My photos were more recent I found, than hers, but they brought her up to date to where I had been for the past sixty-five years and who had arrived in family increases. I had also done the most traveling.

Her photos were stunning. They offered information from the 1800s about our mutual relatives shown in photographs. I instantly saw family resemblances that were inescapable. *So that's who that child looks like!* Not the random appearances I had considered on other sides of the families.

For instance, I had always thought that one of my sons definitely resembled a combination of family members I had selected as possibilities of family traits. The moment I saw a photograph of one of my grandfathers at the age of twenty on his wedding day, I knew that was the image of that son. Even to the body shape, posture and outline of his profile, it was my second son standing in that photograph and the date was 1912. In subsequent photos of that grandfather, I saw the same twinkle, smile and curly hair. It was an emergence of images that was stunning in its ability to reveal inheritances and timing of traits showing themselves in the people born in the same families.

In another time of comparing photos, while visiting one of my husband's aunts' home, I saw a framed picture on the wall of whom I thought was his brother. The only problem was that the person was wearing what looked like one of those stiff celluloid collars of the early 1900s, and a very thick-looking tweed coat. He had a bushy early 1900s mustache which was popular then. I asked someone, "Why is the brother was wearing such old-looking clothes?" and was told that was not the brother, but the grandfather. They were the so-called 'spitting images' of each other. It also amazed me that no one there saw the resemblance. I asked for a copy of the framed picture, took it home and compared it to a similar pose of my husband's brother. They were exactly alike … taken sixty years apart. Even to having the same mustache style.

Do you ever wonder about your own genes? They often can be confused and distracted by known personality traits, but it can be endlessly interesting to chase down those questions about eye colors, body shapes or unquestionable similarities of relatives that somehow get passed along to others. In my three son's linage, it's the eyebrows. They all have their father's family eyebrows.

We all are still waiting for twins to show up for some unsuspecting family. There are multiple sets of those in the past. The most remarkable feature still missing in our linage, though, is my fraternal grandmother's flaming Irish red hair.

It's a Guy Thing

Three brothers who had not all been together with me at the same time, for eighteen years, stood mentally triangulated, taking each other's measure. An odd, inner recognition of one's own kind, stamped and molded each face. One has a good diagnosis of what is happening and is sharing hope and gladness at being together. One is restrained, settled into his regular on-going status of position. Another is quiet, watchful, judging, waiting for moments of acceptance among them, quietly supplying needs in each other's behalf. A servant in physical and emotional goodness.

Each is harboring their own years, wondering how best to relate now, falling back on younger behavior, looking for ways that will not harm while smoothing out the road to experience the affection they have for each other, that is apparent in conversation and looks.

Watching, I see in my mind the young brothers, first grade, Boy Scouts, the teens they were. Now I hear their deep voices, see the gray hairs. I see the wisdom and acceptance of each other as adults, from the distance of those former days.

They tell me stories from the safety of years, already plotting and inventing mythical mischief together, based on former performances from years ago. Each adding a twist to the plot, each still skilled at anticipating the flow of ideas and getting the maximum outcome of expertise and fun to be had in planning and executing imaginary triumphs and mayhem.

I wish I could be within hearing of their serious conversations. I would like to hear how they truly relate to each other now, as grown men. What memories do they share? Where have their hearts gone over the years?

I see the nearness, hope, and happiness at being together, in each face. All of them, at this time, this moment in their lives, are transitioning to new places, divining the future for new directions, new lives and are finally including each other in their plans.

Let them be. Let them find each other again. I sift the memories of them through the filter of my own observations with care of them, responsibility for them, love of them. Now I see them as the men they have become. Each is different and yet the same. I see them find the level of being teens together to find a beginning footing for this new relationship. They progress through those years rapidly and find the metal of each other and their new positions as adults. There is acceptance and respect. Adult conversations sprinkled with the ideas and fun that they suddenly remember and want to tell.

These moments are precious.

LAUGHTER

What is it in us that makes even a small baby roar with laughter? I watched my six month-old being lifted in the air by a friend with layers and layers of red, curly hair, throw his head back when he had his tiny fists buried in her curls and laugh and laugh and laugh. Where does that come from at such a pre-verbal age?

We all know the laugh that catches us off-guard, makes us lose our breath before we can push those explosions of laughter out and leave us helpless and weeping, trying to stop, only to begin again. The feeling bubbles up and it starts all over again. The more spontaneous, the harder it is to then censor ... and it is contagious.

What is going on during grief? My mother had passed away and relatives were coming to Lake Charles, Louisiana for the service. My dad was driving my sister, our grandmother and me around the area to fill time. He was describing the reasons for the graves being above ground in the area because of a high-water table. My sister and I were in the back seat. We looked at each other and knew in an instance what was going to happen. We looked away, trying to hold it in. We strangled, trying to stop what was on its way out. No use. It exploded in great peals of sound that were futile to contain. We tried not to look at each other because that only made it worse. Our elegant, southern grandmother gave us looks from the front seat that under normal circumstances would have left scorch marks where our bodies had been. That only made it worse. I have tried to discover what was going on at that moment. I can say only that it was healing. There obviously is something healing in laughter ... even inappropriate laughter.

But why? And how? It's an activity that almost defies definition or explanation. It's powerful. We can read that it produces endorphins that make us feel good. It can reduce pain and help us past rough spots. It's memorable. We're willing to pay money for comedians to tickle us with their verbal descriptions. How about legendary 'roasts' of celebrities that are deliberate titillations which can cause roars of laughter.

What about someone else's pain? I recently saw an episode on television that featured a chef traveling around the world who was required to eat whatever was offered to him. He admitted to having eaten something disagreeable during that episode and had a segment set up when he was to submit to Asian massage and spa treatments. They included small Mason jars suctioned onto his back and being walked on by tiny Asian women who were also able to contort his body into positions not normally doable. The silent, pleading look on his face was what did me in. I laughed until it was no longer possible to stand up or talk.

We human beings are indeed fearfully, and wonderfully, and strangely made.

Distances of Time
and Place

I have a black and white picture of a young family. They are standing in front of a fence with a billboard, stores, a street off in the distance, behind them. The sun might have been causing a glare because they are all squinting or lowering their heads. The dad is holding a young, curly-haired blond boy, the wife is beside him and two small girls are standing in front of them. They have a 'look' about them. I have often wondered what that 'look' was. Anticipation? There is an energy to it. This seems an important moment to them. There are other pictures with this one family grouping—the girls standing beside a bicycle, the boy alone by the fence. Another, of the mother standing behind the boy with one hand on his shoulder. I would say that they are all dressed for the occasion—the mother wearing a two-piece dress with a clasp of jewelry on her shoulder, the dark lipstick of the era, which I would guess to be in the '40s, the girls in similar dresses—short puffed sleeves and sashes, short white stockings with their white buckled shoes. The boy has a long-sleeved shirt and what looks to be corduroy overalls with the straps crossed in the back and buttoned in the front. The father is dressed in obvious khaki pants and shirt. Possibly a holdover from recently leaving the military?

I found out years later that this indeed was an important picture, an important moment. The father was leaving his family in Venice, California that day to travel to a new opportunity in Oak Ridge, Tennessee. The family would join him later. He had been hired as an electrician, to be part of the ultra-secret Manhattan Project in development there. No one knew what was being built behind the fenced, armed-guarded areas there, only that the wages were good, rentals were provided for a small amount and most facilities for the families were excellent, innovative and free ... and travel was paid for, by the government.

We, as children, were not aware of the plans our parents were making for us. Only that we would be moving soon. We continued our lives as before with the help of relatives. I still took my dimes to school to be put into cards with little slots to hold them, 'for the war effort'. We, as children, had no notion of what was going on in the world. We couldn't know about the battles being fought on the other side of the world, trying to keep Japan and Germany from dominating others ... what our father and other fathers would be working on that would help create an atomic bomb that would change the world forever. We did know how to do the name-calling epitaphs of Tojo, Mussolini and Hitler when we wanted to give a bad label someone. So, some of the essence of the day did manage to seep down into the behavior of the children.

How brave our parents were, to leave all they knew, travel across the country yet again, to work and live in an area, about which, they could be told nothing. I wonder what they talked about in discussing this with others and themselves. I remember that they seemed to be happy with the circumstances there. And there was a great sense of 'community' among the neighbors. My parents kept those same people they met in Oak Ridge, Tennessee, as close friends their whole lives, later living a few miles from each other, when they bought homes in the area after the war was over.

I wonder now what all that newness of other people brought to the area. People from all over the world, working for a common good and then spreading out into the surrounding communities. Communities that had been established here for generations, and now they had to adjust to folks who had not considered their personal history of Civil War, slavery, or southern ideas. I only thought of how I experienced the friends I knew, but I seldom thought about what they had to come to terms with, regarding the people now moving and living amongst them. What were their evaluations of us?

I had heard my fourth-grade school friends whisper to me, my first day of school, "Which side of the Silver War are you on?" I couldn't answer this, never having heard of the Silver War. I asked my dad for an answer when I returned home, and he said, "Just tell them that you are from California." Which was the perfect answer ... but I was now a considered a foreigner.

I can attest to the fact that those circumstances didn't change over the years. There was always a separation, however slight, among my school friends and myself, and as far I as could tell, between my parents and the local people. They still chose their war years friends, who were from all over the states, over the nearest neighbors. The Tennesseans were kind and friendly but didn't necessarily associate with the strangers filtering out into their established areas. The strangers were kindly 'tolerated.'

There were already behaviors and objections in place, such as how they felt about living with and tolerating the Negro people, Catholics and Jewish people living in the area. Catholics were whispered about and quietly identified. I remember being puzzled over the objections they had about the young Catholic girls having pierced ears. This was considered wanton and sinful in those days. But then, I myself was an object of consideration when I wore sleeveless dresses or tops. The Blacks were the most ill-treated of all. In the '40s, they were expected to step off the sidewalk when white people passed.

Seen talking to them was risky and could cause the Ku Klux Klan to burn a cross on your front lawn that night. I saw many of those cross-shaped burned spots from my school bus and then would miss seeing those friends whose families usually quietly left town.

My mother was an accepting Californian, and just treated everyone the same. She made it a point to speak to everyone and make friends with everyone. The Black people began waiting for her on the corners in town because they knew she was always going to stop and chat with them and ask about their families. I could see by the looks on their faces, that they liked her and waited for her to catch up with them. I think she was able to get away with this without anyone rebuking her or burning anything on our lawns because she had an obvious handicap and used it to her advantage. She was pretty sure no one wanted to be accused of harassing someone who had difficulty in walking and had spastic limbs simply because she stopped to speak to people, regardless of their color. Mother was a very smart woman and knew how to use some things to her advantage. And she simply loved people, most of all, when they were needy, misunderstood and especially when they were brave and standing up for the respect they deserved.

I haven't returned to that town too many times, over the years. Nothing has made me want to go back very often, other than curiosity. It's still the same 'steeped in tradition' spot that it always was. The biggest source of friendships were always the people in my school classes. Since I didn't have many relatives, they always felt like my big family of cousins with all their opinions, issues and caring. I love being with them now, as gray and white-haired adults together—we have all softened, having been through our fiery trials, and can now appreciate that we indeed, are an accepting family that did and do care for each other.

MOTHER

How could I have so little memory, at the age of seven, of a train trip from California to Tennessee? None at all, other than my maternal grandmother seeing us off at the terminal. I have a picture in my mind of my 18-month old brother, my four-year-old sister and me with harnesses around our chests and leashes attached so Mother could keep track of us, standing in a group. We must have looked like a little team of Huskies wearing traveling clothes.

Let me explain the leashes. Due to unexplained circumstances when she was a child, my mother became spastic on the entire right side of her body around the age of eighteen months. Until then, her body was perfectly normal. From this distance in time, I can still only admire her brave and adventurous sense of life. That included her continuous creativity in determining how she was going to accomplish things with only one hand, which was sometimes supplemented by the elbow of her spastic right arm. Her way of keeping the three of us in sight and under control was to use dog leashes. It worked, and we all arrived in Tennessee together. I wish I could remember more of the actual three-day train trip such as getting the three of us to the dining car. I do remember my brother passing out each time the train jerked as it began moving after each stop. A kindly doctor recommended sitting him facing towards the front of the train, and that seemed to help.

I can only guess at many challenges my mother overcame because of her handicap. She took her condition for granted and seldom acknowledged it. Our friends would ask, "What is the matter with your mother?"

We would ask them, "What do you mean, what is wrong with our mother?" We really had no concept of her being handicapped. She did everything she wanted to do by adapting whenever she could.

She was an expert patternmaker and sewed most of our clothes. We would show her a style in a magazine, she would put craft paper on the floor, and would cut out a pattern that always fit perfectly. Can you imagine holding material steady, feeding it through a sewing machine, cutting threads, and pressing the seams with only one hand? I have wondered if she had gone to a special school due to her handicap and was taught how to cope with everyday things, plus learn a skill such as sewing so that she could have a profession later in life. It's hard to tell what the procedure might have been for her care and development, since that would have been in the late 1920s. She did woodworking, skated, swam like a fish, kept house, raised three children, and was a notable artist. Dad built a studio for her, probably in the hopes of keeping us two girls out of her materials.

After mother had passed on at age forty-eight, I remember asking my grandmother, "How in the world did she change a diaper? Pick us up? Feed us?"

She said, "To pick you up, your mother would throw you up in the air, catch you and put you on her hip."

"As for the diaper," she said, "We seemed to instinctively hold still until my mother was finished changing them."

That was back when diapers were fabric and folded into three-cornered affairs and had to be pinned on. What a blessing disposable diapers would have been for her! It was amazing to watch her tie our shoestrings. She would pull her little finger out of her right spastic hand which was usually balled up in a fist and would loop one shoestring around that finger and then she would somehow loop another loop around and through that one. They were almost impossible for us to untie. It was a big effort for her, because she had to hold her entire right side still while also kneeling down to reach our shoes.

My mother had many, many strong suits, but cooking was not one of them. We knew what day of the week it was by what was on the table. I think she was very happy that I was interested in cookbooks and would let me make anything I wanted to try. Because of her use of only one hand, stirring grits, sauces or mashing potatoes was done with minimal effort and time, hence my love of lumpy foods.

Mother was a Bohemian-flowerchild before there was such a thing. She was more interested in fleshing out our thoughts, ideas, and opinions than keeping house or cooking. In contrast to her, I was a fussy Martha Stewart prototype, 'it has to be right (at least, according to me), clean it up, keep it moving kind of daughter.' She would often use our washcloths and hand towels to wipe her paint brushes on. I finally hid a set of linens from her that I would set out in the bathroom when guests were coming. What an odd creature she must have thought I was. But in retrospect, she was blessed to have a daughter who would take charge, and I was blessed to have a mother who showed me the world in all its moods and opportunities.

Mother always looked for a straight chair to sit in. She would sit on her spastic hand and wrap her spastic leg around the chair leg. She would then look entirely normal. She had an incredibly open personality and had the ability to make any-one in the world comfortable in her presence. That included a silly-giggle sense of humor that she often fought to control in what were often the oddest situations. You never knew what was going to set her off. She had the cutest crooked smile, which I found out later was due to doctors trying to control the spasms by cutting so many nerves on the right side of her body. They had severed many in her face, so that was the most normal look about her.

There were Negros in the small town we lived in during the '50s who learned to love her. They would wait on corners for her to make her way to them, knowing that she was always going to stop and chat. I was always impatient, wanting to get on with what we had come to do in town, but to her, that was the more important event. I still see the look on their faces. They were friends to her and happy to see her, understanding that being accepted was a struggle for her, too. She carried herself in such an aspect of unawareness of her handicap that others soon could not see it either.

I have pictures of her that show her as a typical young girl with the changing hair styles and clothing that expressed her adolescent need to try on personas in self-discovery. That was made easier by the access to Hollywood studios near her that sold the no longer needed clothing used in movies. In some photos, she is very glamorous, with suits, feathered felt hats and classic heels with a strap. Another one shows her looking over her shoulder wearing a contemporary dress, her hair done in the latest short fashion. Yet another shows her with long hair tied back, a large flower in her hair, a skillfully tied scarf at her neck over a jacket and wearing darker lipstick. I remain fascinated by her willingness and fun at experimenting with personal looks.

My favorite is the one in which she was standing in a fashionably long skirt and was wearing my father's Navy Fleet Champion wrestling sweater. This just before they married in Long Beach, California.

It was 1935 and my dad was stationed in San Diego, California aboard the battleship USS Mississippi when he met my mother in a skating rink. I really don't have a lot of information regarding those days, and there are only a few photos to ponder.

Mother had three older sisters and a younger brother. I can only wonder at the dynamics of their childhoods. Her father passed away shortly after her brother was born and as often happened in those war years, children were sent to live with relatives when there were difficult family problems. Grandmother sent the two oldest girls, Cora Lee and Bertie, to live with aunts, keeping my mother, Margaret, who was handicapped, her brother Dan, who was the youngest and the next youngest daughter, Lorraine, with her. Judging from photographs, the family seems to be dressed in the latest fashions with hair styles are up-to-date and changed often. Those photos and the stories heard over the years lead me to understand they had a comfortable and well-cared for life.

I can only guess at what Mother's physical circumstances were like. She obviously received medical attention to control the spastic state on one side of her body as surgeries to sever nerves that caused the worst contractions. I have one photo taken of her and one of her sisters when she was 18 months old and still had normal use of her body. Whatever the physical illness was that struck her happened shortly after the photo was made.

I now believe she might have attended a facility that treated her physical problems and taught her life-affirming skills. Mother never mentioned such a thing, but she was too skilled in all that she did. I wonder if she had been taught to be a seamstress and patternmaker as part of a preparation given to her for a life so she could take care of herself. The attitudes about her handicap, I believe, came naturally to her and the ability to minimally acknowledge her limitations. Indeed, she acted as though they didn't exist.

To describe Mother's physical differences, I would have to tell someone that her right leg was a little shorter than the left, due to the spasms. The entire right side of her body was uncontrollably spastic. That would include every muscle she had on that side. For instance, her right arm—if she didn't restrain or immobilize it somehow, it would naturally curl up into a tight knot at her side. She could control its movement for a short time, for instance, when she had to hold something down or tie our shoelaces. That was the reason she sat on her right hand most of the time. Also, her right leg would have spasms if not kept under control, so she would wrap it around a chair leg. The right side of her face would sometimes grimace, but most of those nerves had been severed to create a more normal look. Because she had taught herself to control or ignore the problems her body was trying to give her, most of the time she looked entirely normal. Occasionally, her right hand would twist out and grab someone's clothing or arm, but she invariably made everyone comfortable by laughing and untangling everything, all while explaining what had happened and why.

Apparently, the circumstances of the children of my mother's family who were separated did not diminish their closeness either then or as they aged. Somehow, they kept in touch with each other, because as I knew them over the years, and they were always close.

My dad was born and raised around Palm Beach, Florida but spent part of his early years in New York City. His father's family was involved in building boats, but their business mostly ran aground during the Great Depression. Dad was a natural storyteller, and I gather from most of the family, that he was a bit of a rascal.

His mother was a true, gracious Southern lady whose family lived in Richmond, Virginia. I still remember her lovely summer dresses, lightly flowing and often made of a fabric called "lawn." Her clothes were always hand-made, either by a seamstress or herself. When she came to visit, years later, we would save a quiet moment for the two of us, and as I would sit beside her, she unpacked her small suitcase and showed me each piece. She would gently turn up the hems so I could see the beautiful tiny stitches, and she would explain the mechanics of making the dress. The family was well-off enough financially, so they often spent part of the winters in Havana, Cuba when it was safe and fashionable to do so in the 1920s. My maternal great-grandfather was mayor of Del Ray Beach, Florida when I first met him.

As mentioned before, Dad was stationed in San Diego, California working as a radio-operator aboard the USS Mississippi battleship, when he met Mother in a skating rink. After they married, he took her to Jupiter, Florida where mother was meant to stay with his parents while he finished his enlistment, before being discharged from the military. He was then stationed on the East coast. The friendship between Mother and her new in-laws was less than perfect, especially when someone began to intercept her allotment payments from the Navy. She determined it was her father-in-law. Too teach him a lesson, she sneaked up behind him with a ball peen hammer with intentions to bang him on the head. Fortunately, someone noticed what was happening and intervened. Well, that initiated a visit from Dad, and while I don't know what happened exactly, I do know that Mother left and went back to California and Dad back to his ship.

At some point after the Florida visit, my Dad was hit on the head by one of the hatch covers on a ship during a drill. That caused him to have occasional seizures, so he was given a medical discharge from the US Navy. He was able, through the help of a relative, to find work in New York City as an electrician in a hotel.

Now, whoever knows what lies in the future? Mother discovered that she was pregnant and took the next bus from California to New York City to join him.

All I have visually of those years are a few pictures taken on my first birthday, standing outside on a sidewalk and sitting on the brownstone stairs where my parents lived in Brooklyn. I am wearing high-topped shoes laced up with the stockings turned down over the shoe tops, a little dress and short curly hair. In one of the photos, I am sitting on my dad's knee with Mother beside us.

I've been told stories of my mother's first delivery, and that because of her spastic physical condition and being pregnant, she had a special team of doctors at the hospital who all wanted to be part of a unique situation. I do think she liked the extra attention.

One of her stories involved the use of Jell-O being added to all my baby food to create an incentive to eat. Later, when this appeared to be a problem, a child should not have Jell-O consistently added to their food and drinks, the doctor suggested that she starve me out of the habit. That was our first contest of wills. She obviously won, because I am now still Jell-O-free.

Before the age of eighteen months, I developed pneumonia. I was put up on the roof of the hospital and wrapped in blankets, in the snow, in an effort to bring the temperature down. Twice. Apparently, a Catholic priest gave me the Last Rites at some point. After my return home, my parents decided the next best thing to do was to move to West Palm Beach, Florida.

My Medical Career

I think I was about eight years old, when I did my first 'touch-less suturing job.' My parents had left me in charge of babysitting my two-year-old brother and five-year-old sister. My brother somehow had cut the end of one of his toes off and hopped to me with it dangling by a tiny piece of skin. I thought I was going to be in 'Big Trouble' if I didn't come up with a remedy. I got him into the bathroom, cleaned him up and put a big piece of tape around it. That seemed to work well. My brother stopped wailing and was stumping around, admiring his white toe. I told my parents that he had hurt his toe, hence the tape. I guess they just kept changing the bandage because I don't remember them saying anything. To this day, my brother still shows me the little bump on the end of one of his toes.

Another time of baby-sitting (same ages) my sister was running with a popsicle stick in her mouth. She came running to me with this thing sticking in the roof of her mouth! I yanked it out and got her something to drink. She seemed to be OK, so I didn't mention that visit to my infirmary to my parents. It was so odd. Years later she told me about not being able to have some specific dental work done 'due to a large lump on the roof of her mouth.' It was then that I thought to tell her what I had done that day. She had just been assuming that all people had lumps there. I must have done a good job since no dentist ever told her, either. Did I mention she had a beautiful voice and sang in nightclubs for a time? Surely my medical expertise had something to do with that.

Around that same year one of our aunts came to visit. And as usual, my parents were gone when a medical emergency came up. She accidentally stuck her fingers into an oscillating fan and cut two or three of them. Back into the bathroom we went with my roll of tape. I think I knew how to use gauze by that time. My parents were becoming very proud of my work. I can still see that aunt with her three bandaged fingers sticking out. I tended to use quite a bit of tape and gauze back then.

Then there was my dad. He was forever whacking or cutting himself with something, being a do-it-himselfer. Once, the head of a pickax came off while he was digging something outside and it hit his head. Mom called me to come help. That injury truly needed stitching, and I definitely wasn't up to that part of my medical experience yet. And it was beyond tape and gauze. I did drive him (I was fourteen) to the only doctor in town who took care of it. That winter a kerosene heater in the house exploded, and he saved us by carrying it outside. He had terrible third degree burns on that side of his body. I again drove him to the doctors. It was a Sunday and there was no other medical facility around. The doctor did not want to spend time cleaning the petroleum product off his skin. He told me to take him back home and wash the burned areas. I have seldom in my life been that physically angry at someone. I did demand that he give my dad something for shock because even at that age I could see that he was not doing well. No hope for it. I took Dad back home where mother and I gently washed those areas, then back to the doctor's office so he would finally take care of him.

Over the years there have always been emergencies with my children with skinned knees, broken arms and teeth knocked loose by bike falls. Fortunately, there weren't too many of those. I don't know whether they were becoming more careful, or I was becoming wilier in prevention care. In any case, I can still do a mean bandage.

Memories

Have you ever tried to get back to the moment of your own first consciousness … the very first thought that you had, that you were aware of? Not just snippets of memory, but the moment that you were aware of being you. How far could you get? Two years old? Two-and-a-half? Three?

I was on my hands and knees, no shirt, only short pants. I can feel the soft sun filtering through the palm trees that are resulting in a little breeze and making changing shapes on the ground.

I am in the front yard—house to my left, sidewalks and street to the right and I am dragging my tongue in the sand. It's white and looked as though it would taste like sugar. Disgust and shock. It was dry, gritty and hard to get out of my mouth. I'm not sure how I got rid of it. How could I have been so wrong?

Our house was a block from the Catholic hospital where my sister would be born. Mother would often take me to the end of the driveway and point to the hospital and say that she was going there to have a baby and it would come home with her.

This just seemed all 'matter of fact' to me. No big deal. I took it upon myself several times to ride my tricycle across the West Palm Beach Highway and look around this place mother was going to be. I remember the nuns outside asking me where I lived.

I don't remember Mother being aware of this. She was probably slow-moving, being only four-foot-ten-inches and eight-plus months pregnant. She was also paralyzed and spastic on the right side of her body, but I never noticed that slowing her down.

Once on one of my trike tours, I found a balloon in the street tied in a knot. I tried to un-tie it with my teeth and bit a hole in it. Never did that again.

Mother would fill a little bucket with water, which was big enough for me to sit in up to my neck, and I would hunker down in there and observe the world from my little cool spot. There were bushes nearby that had hard berries. I was told not to eat them, so I stuffed my ears full.

Mother finally brought my sister home. Her crib was in their bedroom, and I was determined to climb in and sit with her. She was tiny, dark-haired. All I can really recall is her little rump covered with a diaper, sticking up in the air. Always sleeping.

I returned to this house in the '80s. It was easy to locate because the hospital was still across the street. The house was derelict. Windows broken, boards falling off, grimy, trash everywhere.

But I could see through a window the bedroom where the crib had been, where a relationship that has spanned many decades began.

Bachelor Survival Training

"I don't care if they ARE boys! They are still going to learn to take care of their spaces. This is my ruling, as my own mother used to say, and I am sticking to it."

That was an internal discussion I had with myself about the time my three boys became old enough to create enough debris that it took longer and longer to deal with it. There had been on-site discussions about aim and velocity in the bathrooms resulting in the removal of the rug around the toilet and a groan-producing decision about the short-term removal of the shower curtain after buying several curtains due to the consistent imprints of greasy handprints. Two of the boys were becoming interested in tinkering with cars and wiped on whatever was convenient. I WAS grateful that they voluntarily took showers, and object lessons were important. But ... the result was black rings around the tub. The feeling was, I can't win.

The two oldest were so adorable when they were three and five, standing on chairs at the kitchen sink, chatting quietly while they finished washing the plastic containers and lids for me. They looked forward to it then. Now I found those same containers and lids all around the house, crusty and disagreeable. Very much as their Mom was becoming.

I thought back to the days when my mother taught us life-affirming lessons in self-care. That included separating clothes to wash, washing clothes in the machine, handwashing clothes, hanging clothes outside on lines, folding clothes and putting them away, keeping beds made and bedrooms clean. Helping in the kitchen included setting the table, clearing the table, and washing and drying dishes. Later, she taught us how to do banking, send money orders (people did that back then), make shopping lists, go along to the store with her, and discuss the size, shape and cost of items.

Yes, it was time. I sat them down one evening and explained they were now old enough, and they would enter Bachelor Survival Training each Saturday. It would include helping with dusting, vacuuming, polishing furniture, carrying clothes down to the laundry (I would wash them for now), cleaning their bedrooms, and putting their things away. Dad would show them the joys of outside training, including mowing and raking the yard and washing cars. Mild groaning and muttering were heard, but no matter, they saw the conviction in their mom's eyes and voice. They actually got into the routine with rhythm and expectations of each Saturday by becoming proficient and speedy. I gently added additional items such as coming down to fold their own clothing, carry them to their rooms to put away and scrubbing bathrooms. A subtle rebellion of sorts began to show up, such as things stuffed into their closets and under beds. The rooms looked neat but there was chaos in highly and tightly stacked clutter where it could not be seen. There was unfinished food in dishes behind their beds with the scent of unwashed socks and gym underwear curling down the hallways. My plans were slowly dissolving under the assault of teenage hormones and attitudes.

The five-year-old was easy to reckon with. His room was always messy with toys and games, but he was good about throwing a blanket over the bed and putting the pillow at the right end. The oldest boy could be bargained with, 'no cleanee, no eatee.' He had a raving appetite, and food was a definite incentive. Not that I would have withheld anything from him, but he understood the concept. Try to have it done by dinner time.

My middle son was my waterloo. He was easy-going, twinkled when he smiled and cleaned his room so immaculately that I was tempted to put it on display. When he did it. There began an insidious layer of items. Here and there… lying about on chairs, desk, floor, bed. It was hard to fuss at him; he was so agreeable. "Yes, Mom, I'll do it now … Later … Tonight … Tomorrow … Next year." That continued until I saw that he had to kick his way into the room via things on the floor.

So help me, I could no longer hold it in. I raked everything out of his closet which was filled to overflowing with unhung clothes, shoes, school papers and books into a pile in the middle of the room. I took everything off the surfaces and added them to the heap. Then I pulled the mattress off the bed, which had not been made in a week, and piled it on the top of it all, like a huge, thick, material sandwich top.

When he returned from school, I heard him walk down the hall, open his door and say, "Oh Mom," and sigh. He put it all back together into the good order that he was capable of and was good natured about it all.

I never did that again, but we reached an understanding that day. Moms have limits, too. I had told them that one of the benefits of BST was that hopefully they would get married some day because they wanted to, not because they had to have someone take care of them.

That was my ruling and I stuck to it.

About the Author

Diane Cone Torgersen was born in Brooklyn, New York. Her parents moved between New York, Florida, California and Tennessee during her school years. She attended the School of Radiologic Technology in Charlotte, North Carolina. Over the next few years, she married and moved to Texas, Alaska and finally settled near Annapolis, Maryland. During that time, she and her husband spent three years in Cheltenham, England, with their three sons. While living there, she attended the Gloucestershire College of Art and Design and was privileged to have taught private design classes in needlepoint and embroideries.

Later in life, Diane remarried and continued studying art and interior design, working in those areas for a number of years in the Annapolis and Rehoboth Beach areas. She and her husband later moved to Florida where she continued art and Sumi-e oriental painting classes and began designing art pillows. She became known as 'The Pillow Lady' up and down the east coast of Florida, while also continuing to work in fine art. She ultimately moved to Wilmington, North Carolina where she began to add wall-hangings and painted canvas rugs to her inventory of pillow designs.

Diane aspired to be a writer since writing essays in the third grade, two of which she still has. She has always had a strong thread of writing throughout her life, while pursuing other interests and careers involving fine arts, small entrepreneurship's, and painted fiber arts.

Diane's signature entry into the writing world began when she joined the Landfall Writers Group in Wilmington, North Carolina in 2015. She found she had a strong voice in writing reflective humor. Her stories are mostly drawn from childhood, her observations, raising a family and simply living – all done with an ability to tell stories from another viewpoint and reinterpret special moments.

To her delight, Diane has been published in both books and magazines.